Schools Where Everyone Belongs

Practical Strategies for Reducing Bullying

SECOND EDITION

Stan Davis
with Julia Davis

Research Press
2612 North Mattis Avenue, Champaign, Illinois 61822
(800) 519-2707
www.researchpress.com

Composition by Jeff Helgesen
Cover design by Linda Brown, Positive I.D. Graphic Design, Inc.
Printed by McNaughton & Gunn, Inc.

ISBN-13: 978–0–87822–584–2
ISBN-10: 0–87822–584–6

Library of Congress Control Number 2006933938

To my dear children, Max and Julia, who have taught me about imagination, determination, openness to all people, and the power of being yourself. May your children grow up in a world free of bullying.

Where, after all, do universal human rights begin? In small places, close to home—so close and so small that they cannot be seen on any map of the world. Yet they are the world of the individual person: the neighborhood he lives in; the school or college he attends; the factory, farm or office where he works. Such are the places where every man, woman and child seeks equal justice, equal opportunity, equal dignity without discrimination. Unless these rights have meaning there, they have little meaning anywhere. Without concerted citizen action to uphold them close to home, we shall look in vain for progress in the larger world.

—Eleanor Roosevelt (1884–1962)

CONTENTS

PREFACE

I wrote the first edition of *Schools Where Everyone Belongs* to spread the word about ideas and techniques that work to prevent bullying. Since I began writing the book in 2002, I have continued to travel and talk with parents, educators, and students about bullying. In this new edition, I address the most frequent questions and concerns of those who have participated in my workshops and read the first edition of this book.

Specifically, I have added chapter 18, "Preventing Disability Harassment," in response to the concerns of parents and advocates who told me about how the young people they help are mistreated, both verbally and physically. Also entirely new is an appendix devoted to guiding questions for the development and implementation of successful discipline programs, contributed by my friend and colleague Dee Lindenberger, trainer for the Marquette-Alger Regional Education Service Agency and the Michigan Strategic Alternatives in Prevention Education (SAPE) Association. She is a co-developer of Bully-Free Schools (www.sape.us).

In addition to updates throughout the book, I have supplemented chapter 11, "A Rubric-Based Discipline System," with a troubleshooting guide for school discipline systems designed to answer frequently asked questions about rubric-based discipline. Chapter 12, "Helping Young People Take Responsibility for Their Behavior," now includes a set of guidelines for using the reflection process effectively.

I rewrote chapter 16, "Activating Peer Bystanders," to reflect new research and my continuing experiences of talking with young people. It presents what I believe is a more effective approach to this important element of bullying prevention, which will be the subject of my upcoming book, *From Sympathy to Action: Empowering Peer Bystanders in Bullying Prevention.*

I hope this new edition answers my readers' and workshop participants' main questions. I also hope that it continues to affirm my belief that schools can be a safe place for everyone—and that the dialogue continues. I thank all the people who have worked with me to apply and clarify these ideas.

ACKNOWLEDGMENTS

Any book is the product of many people working together. This one was made possible by the work of the researchers who have taught me so much, first among them Dr. Dan Olweus. Special thanks to Dorothea Ross and Susan Limber for their encouragement.

My daughter, Julia Davis, edited this book, helping me pour the verbal storytelling of my training program onto the printed page, pointing out inconsistencies and errors, and helping me find a narrative voice. She contributed her deep insights about making schools more inclusive and saved me from many incidents of fuzzy reasoning.

The gifted, committed, and empathic staff at the James H. Bean School, and in all the schools I have worked with, helped me develop and test methods and procedures and told me what didn't work. You all helped me move these techniques into teachable form. I have learned so much from watching all of you at work!

The young people I have counseled and talked with about bullying have shared the reality of their lives with me and have helped me see that change is possible.

My seminar students have implemented, questioned, clarified, and extended the work in this book. I am blessed to have worked with you.

My deepest thanks also to Ben Alper, who showed me and so many others the power of mentoring, and to the many librarians who made this book possible:

- To my elementary school librarian, who let me work shelving books when I needed a way to escape the bullies on the playground, after every other adult at my school had told me: "You have to go out and face them."

- To Janet and Sandra, who helped me find articles and books through interlibrary loan.

- To the friendly librarians at the Jesup Library in Bar Harbor, who let Julia store her laptop there and use the Internet connection to e-mail edited chapters back and forth.

- Most of all, to Jane, the librarian I am married to, for showing me every day the true meaning of kindness and acceptance.

INTRODUCTION

BUILDING CARING SCHOOLS

I work in the future. I look at the children passing by in my elementary school and wonder about the lives they will lead as adults. As I travel around the United States talking about bullying, I meet many more young people. Some are resilient, happy, and energetic. Others are clingy, angry, and easily discouraged. Most are happy, productive young people. Some hurt others and are unlikely to succeed in life unless families and educators help them change.

Fifteen years ago, after a career in hospitals, community mental health centers, and private practice as a child and family therapist, I went back to college to become a school counselor. I did this because I was convinced that a positive school experience is a fundamental factor that can make a difference for high-risk youth. School is a place where young people can experience the joys of working hard toward a significant goal, make friends, learn to work and play with others, and learn who they are. A good school can provide a supportive, corrective experience for young people who have lost their way.

School is also where most bullying takes place. This is not because schools cause bullying but because school is the place where children are thrown together with others with whom they ordinarily would not choose to spend time. Bullying will happen when children are together in large groups, especially if adults don't supervise closely.

1

In my career as a therapist, I worked with many targets of bullying. I found that nothing I had been trained to do helped them very much. As many of us do, I tried to help these young people feel good about themselves. I encouraged them to ignore the bullying and not show that it was bothering them. I taught them to be assertive and use I-messages. I remember one young man in particular whom I coached to stand up for himself. He showed up in my office the next week with a black eye. "I don't like your advice," he said.* I realized that I too no longer believed in the advice I was giving youth. Bullies themselves rarely appeared in my office. I found that they were, for the most part, comfortable with their own behavior and willing to put up with occasional punishments in exchange for the feelings of power they got from intimidating others.

When I became a school counselor I continued to attempt to support targets of bullying, and I began talking with bullies more often. Listening to both groups of young people, I began my search for more effective interventions for this problem. The first obstacles I came across were the assumptions and misperceptions that many people hold in regard to bullying. Children's fiction, TV, movies, and other aspects of popular culture have a great influence on our thinking about bullying. In the vast majority of children's books and movies about bullying, the target struggles to find a way to stop the bullying. No one helps him or her. Finally the target stands up to the bully by learning karate, putting hot sauce in a sandwich she knows the bully is going to steal, hitting the bully, or yelling. After this, the bully goes away, or even becomes friends with the target. In real life, standing up to bullies can sometimes solve the problem. It can also cause the target to be hit, kicked, humiliated, or punished.

---

* Note: All the stories in this book are true, and the dialogue within them is as accurate as memory allows. I have changed names and identifying details.

Then there's the expression "Sticks and stones may break my bones, but words will never hurt me." As I have traveled around the United States talking with almost 40,000 young people about bullying, I say the first two words of this sentence and stop. In Ohio, Missouri, New Hampshire, Southern California, Florida, Massachusetts, and Maine, young people chant the rest of the sentence back to me. Young people all over the United States seem to have learned this message by heart. What exactly are we telling young people when we give them this advice? Most adults have experienced some kind of physical injury in their lives and subsequently many have forgotten the details. Many of us do remember with deep pain something humiliating that a parent, friend, or teacher said to us many years ago. Do we really believe that ignoring bullying negates the effect it has on students? Denying the reality of painful feelings does not help people overcome their pain. It can, instead, stop them from taking action to change the situation. To look at an analogy, suppose that Martin Luther King Jr., instead of mobilizing people to end segregation, had used his skills as a leader to tell African Americans, "Don't let segregation bother you." How would our world be different?

I came to believe that bullying was inevitable. Then, in 1996, something happened that changed my outlook. I was working as a counselor in a small rural school in Maine. A group of boys had been teasing and excluding one student at the school. The target's parents threatened to sue the school district if the school didn't find a way to stop the harassment. I tried what I knew how to do. I tried talking with the target about not reacting so strongly, talking with the bullies about the impact of their behavior, and offering the target other places to be during recess and lunch. None of these actions made a difference.

Pressured by the target's parents, the principal and I again surveyed the research and found Dan Olweus's book, *Bullying at School: What We Know and What We Can Do* (1993). I also read Dorothea Ross's book, *Childhood Bullying and Teasing* (1996), and learned about Wendy Craig and Debra Pepler's observational research in Canada. It was Dr. Olweus who had the greatest impact on my work, by outlining a research-based intervention that reduced rates of bullying by 50 percent or more in schools in Norway. The principal and I began implementing parts of the Olweus program.

We provided training for all staff. We arranged small, inevitable, and consistent consequences for any acts of name-calling, hitting, or systematic exclusion. We talked with all the students about their responsibilities when observing bullying. We recognized students' acts of reaching out to unpopular peers. We educated parents. Reports of bullying at the school decreased dramatically, both for the child we were most concerned about and for the other students as well.

I realized how well Dr. Olweus's work fit with my own training in family and organizational dynamics, which has taught me that changing a system is more likely to lead to real and durable change than changing an individual.

Several years later I moved to the school where I work now. Building on Dr. Olweus's research and working with the caring, creative group of teachers and principals at the James H. Bean School, in Sidney, Maine, I have developed a set of specific, teachable techniques for increasing the effectiveness of disciplinary approaches, modeling positive behavior, helping aggressive youth change, supporting targets, and empowering bystanders. As we have implemented and added to our bullying prevention program since 1998, we have seen dramatic and continuing reductions in student reports of bullying. From 1998 to 2005, our fifth graders reported an 84 percent reduction in physical bullying, an 83 percent reduction in teasing, and a 75 percent reduction in exclusion. More evaluation data about the Bean school intervention can be found on-line at http://www.stopbullyingonw.com/Bean9905.pdf. I will continue to post program updates and evaluation data on the stopbullyingnow.com Web site.

Our students tell us they feel safe and comfortable in our school every day. Here are three of the many stories I could tell:

Two brothers moved to our school from a nearby city. They had shaggy hair and threadbare clothes and clearly came from a family that was struggling financially. The counselor at their school called before they arrived to let me know that they regularly missed two or three days of school every month. He described their home as somewhat disorganized and told me I would have to set up a reward system to encourage them to consistently attend school. I noticed, though, that they were at school almost every day. After a month of perfect attendance, I asked the older brother why they were at school so much more. "No one teases us here," he said. "At our old school we were teased every day."

A boy moved to town in the middle of his fifth grade year. By the age of 11 he had already been diagnosed with bipolar disorder and posttraumatic stress disorder. In his old school he had thrown desks and other heavy objects at other childrens' heads. At our school peers welcomed him, did not tease him about the stuffed animals he brought to school, and played with him. During his year and a half with us he never hit another student. I asked him why he had changed his behavior. He looked at me as if surprised and said, "You don't let people hit here."

When we began our intervention, Darla was the target of consistent harassment by her third grade class. Uncoordinated, overweight, and easily provoked to tears, she had no friends and often provoked negative attention. Darla often came to adults to tell them about having been hit, slapped, called names, and excluded. The harassment came from about half of the

third grade class. It seemed that most of the class had agreed
that she was an easy scapegoat, and teasing her won the
approval of the class. Three years later, the harassment had
stopped. Darla had friends. She had developed a more posi-
tive view of herself and better social skills. She returned for a
visit after a year in middle school to tell me that the students
who had been at the Bean school with her, even those who had
harassed her in the lower grades, helped her make friends in
middle school and protected her from other peers if she was
harassed.

As we further defined strategies that work in bullying prevention, I set up a web site to share the techniques we were developing.
Our school was featured in magazines, on television, and on the radio.
I began getting invitations to train staff at other schools. Now I spend
three days a week at the Bean school and two days a week on the
road. My travels have taken me all over the United States and this
year I begin training schools in Canada. I am writing this book to
continue to spread the word that bullying can be stopped.

I also write this book to thank the many educators who make
a difference every day in the lives of young people. Many wonderful teachers, librarians, and other educators taught, nurtured,
and helped me survive my own childhood. I see educators saving
students' lives every day. I believe that our work in schools can
make a difference in the future of children and ultimately the future
of our society.

We are the hope for youth, and a society, at risk. As James
Garbarino (1999) writes in *Lost Boys,*

> [A significant] foundation for resilience is social sup-
> port from persons or institutions outside the family.
> Social support has at least two distinct dimensions.
> The first is its role in making the individual feel con-

nected to people beyond the confines of the family.
The second is its role in promoting prosocial behavior. . . . Kids who live in dysfunctional families . . .
may have nowhere to turn to receive positive messages about themselves and learn about mainstream
values. . . . Schools [are] potentially the one place to
provide the warm, firm embrace [a youth at risk]
needs. (p. 168)

I will write in this book about mistakes educators and counselors make. I want to stress from the beginning that *these mistakes
are all mistakes I have made myself.* My hope in sharing errors is
not to criticize schools or teachers, but rather to encourage people
who work with young people to look critically at their own behavior. The first and least expensive way to make change is to stop our
behavior that makes things worse. I think of an anonymous quote
I once saw posted above a chalkboard. It stated: "It is acceptable
to make mistakes in this classroom. All I ask is that you do your
best to make a different mistake each time."

This book is organized sequentially. After a brief discussion of
bullying and its effects, I will present techniques and structures that
improve school safety and climate. I am convinced that bullying
prevention is primarily something we *do* rather than something we
teach. Our actions in reacting to bullying, connecting with youth,
and modeling positive behavior are the foundation of bullying prevention. Interventions to help aggressive youth internalize rules
and develop conscience come next, paired with methods for helping targets heal. The last section of the book addresses schoolwide
educational interventions and other methods for empowering
bystanders to act against bullying, which are most effective when
built on a foundation of staff intervention and modeling.

When effective disciplinary interventions and positive adult
modeling are in place, bystanders can feel safe in discouraging

bullying, just as neighborhood watch programs can be effective when based on prompt police response and protection.

At the end of each chapter I have suggested further reading. The books and articles in the bibliography are all useful resources for extending your skills. Finally, I look forward to hearing from you about your questions, your reactions, and the new techniques you develop as you work to prevent bullying.

You can reach me at stan@stopbullyingnow.com. I will be adding new and revised ideas, posting your letters, and continuing to list new resources and research at http://www.stopbullyingnow.com/bookadditions.htm. I invite you to contribute to this growing conversation and to visit the site for more information.

CHAPTER 1

WHAT IS BULLYING?

Bullying is a form of social interaction—not necessarily long-standing—in which a more dominant individual (the bully) exhibits aggressive behavior that is intended to, and does, in fact, cause distress to a less dominant individual (the victim). The aggressive behavior may take the form of a direct physical and/or verbal attack or may be indirect. More than one bully and more than one victim may participate in the interaction.

—Dorothea Ross (1996)

My own understanding of bullying comes primarily from my own experiences, the many young people I have counseled, the adults who have told me their own stories, the almost 40,000 young people who have attended my workshops, and the many students who have written to me afterward. They have given me the following picture. Bullies tease, hit, threaten, start rumors about, and/or otherwise harass targets. They pressure others to keep silent about the bullying and to exclude targets from friendship. Bullies experience a wish for power that is stronger than their empathic sense, so they are willing to hurt others in order to feel powerful. As Dorothea Ross (1996) points out, young people who bully enjoy the power they have over their victims and do not bully in order to receive tangible rewards, such as lunch money. Instead, bullies focus on behaviors that will hurt or embarrass their targets.

> Bullying is about power.

Youth who bully often deny what they have done, minimize the significance of the bullying, or blame their actions on others' behavior. They threaten bystanders in order to keep them quiet and accept consequences only reluctantly, while maintaining that they did nothing wrong or that the target deserved it. A notorious high school bully, whom I later learned had terrorized classmates for years, said in a recent workshop of mine, "The problem is that people don't have a sense of humor. They should just learn to take a little teasing."

> Bullies choose targets with little social support.

Bullies choose targets who have little social support. As a teen in San Diego told me, "They find someone who has no backup." Then they look for attributes of the chosen target that they can use to justify harassment. Maybe the target is skinny, fat, wears glasses, or is Jewish, Muslim, or smart. If bullies can't find a way in which the target is different, they invent one. They make it clear to their target and to bystanders that attributes of the target form the basis for the harassment. They use phrases such as "He's a geek," "Those pants are so gay," "Hitler had the right idea about Jews," and "Suzie's a slut." Targets may try standing up to bullies alone. Bullies may then shift their harassment to another target, or they may intensify the harassment to emphasize their power. Targets may try to ignore the bully. Again, bullies may then shift the harassment to another target or may try harder to get a response.

Some research about bullying focuses on the personality characteristics of targets. Targets of bullying, we are often told, lack self-confidence. "[P]assive victims of bullying generally signal, through their behavior and attitudes, that they are a bit anxious and unsure of themselves" (Olweus, 2003a, p. 8). This lack of self-confidence, as Dr. Olweus points out in his article, could also be a result of bullying.

Additional research about bullying points out other characteristics of targets. Sweeting and West (2001) found that youth who are less physically attractive; overweight; have a disability such as a sight, hearing, or speech problem; and perform poorly at school are more likely to be bullied. In their article, they write: "Characteristics of appearance, disability, or ability which in themselves may be difficult to deal with also increase the likelihood that a child will experience the additional burden of being bullied" (p. 2).

Other groups of students are likely to be bullied, especially young people who are gay or lesbian or who are perceived to be outside a narrow definition of masculinity or femininity. Teens around the United States have told me that the most common insults they experience relate to gender roles. They are called "gay," "lesbians," "sluts," "pussies."

Kimmel and Mahler (2003) found in their review of school shootings:

> In conducting our analysis, we found a striking pattern from the stories about the boys who

committed the violence: Nearly all had stories of
being constantly bullied, beat up, and, most significantly for this analysis, "gay-baited." Nearly
all had stories of being mercilessly and constantly
teased, picked on, and threatened. And most strik-
ingly, it was not because they were gay (at least
there is no evidence to suggest that any of them
were gay) but because they were different from
the other boys—shy, bookish, honor students,
artistic, musical, theatrical, nonathletic, "geek-
ish," or weird. Theirs are stories of "cultural mar-
ginalization" based on criteria for adequate gender
performance, specifically the enactment of codes
of masculinity. (p. 7)

Similarly, Brown (2003) writes:

Unfortunately, girls often gain power by using the
tools of sexism on each other in ways that maintain the broader patriarchal landscape, such as using
the language of sexual objectification—calling
other girls hos, sluts, and bitches—or judging other
girls and women against narrow images of beauty.
Interrupting girlfighting means advocating for gender diversity—for many ways to be girls of sub-
stance—and offering girls opportunities to try on
different identities, to experience more visible
avenues to power, to challenge sexist, racist, homo-
phobic arrangements, to feel in control and to create environments that feel good to them. This won't
get rid of all girlfighting and shouldn't—girls
should be encouraged to feel angry and fight in
constructive ways about the things that really matter to them. But I believe it will work to reduce the
misogynistic forms of girlfighting that so prevail
in our culture. (p. 3)

Brown's recommendations about addressing class, gender, and race issues in bullying prevention can be found in Brown (2006), *Creating Safe, Responsive Schools.*

Bystanders tell me they often watch in silence or laugh nervously. Bullies interpret this silence and laughter as a sign of approval. Peers distance themselves from targets of bullying, often believing what bullies say about their targets, and equally often wanting to protect themselves from harassment through association.

People often ask me if aggression is an expression of bullies' low self-esteem. Students tell me that "bullies are unhappy people who are jealous of their targets." I have found no research evidence to support these views, nor does my experience talking with bullies support them. I have found most bullies to be self-confident and comfortable with their actions. Research from Olweus (2003a, 2003b); Baumeister, Bushman, and Campbell (2000); Baumeister (2001); and Baumeister, Campbell, Krueger, and Vohs (2003) directly contradicts the ideas that aggressive youth have low self-esteem and that improving self-esteem will lead to less aggressive behavior.

As I continue to talk with young people about the belief that bullies are unhappy people who are "just jealous," I ask how many of *them* have been unhappy or jealous or have had problems at home. The majority of the students in the audience raise their hands. How many of them, I ask, have dealt with those feelings without intimidating, harassing, or hurting others? Most of the students raise their hands again.

Juvonen, Graham, and Schuster (2003) found in their study of 1,985 sixth graders that bullies were less likely than nonbullies, and significantly less likely than targets of bullying, to show signs of depression, social anxiety, or loneliness. They also found that "bullies were regarded as highest,

> Most bullies are happy and self-confident. Many bullies are popular.

and victims the lowest in social status [by peers]. . . . Teacher ratings indicated that bullies were most popular and victims least popular" (p. 1233). As these researchers point out, as long as peers reward bullying behavior with high social status, bullies are likely to continue that behavior. We need to work with bystanders to help them see that bullying is cowardly rather than heroic.

Young people are more likely to bully if adults and peers see their behavior and do nothing to stop it, in effect showing their approval. Young people are even more likely to bully if adults model or encourage bullying behavior. I remember once being at an amusement park with a group of sixth graders, when a group from another school showed up to use the bumper cars. One teacher climbed into his car, yelling, "Everybody get Kevin!" The other students joined in despite the fact that Kevin showed no signs that he was enjoying being the target of their continuing teasing.

I look at bullying in another way as well—through the lens of a trained therapist. In my training I was taught to make a useful distinction between ego-syntonic and ego-dystonic behaviors. Ego-syntonic behaviors are comfortable for the person performing the behavior. These behaviors are seen as an expression of the person's beliefs and life goals. Ego-dystonic behaviors are those with which the person feels uncomfortable. These behaviors are seen as contrary to the person's values and beliefs. Most counseling approaches are focused on helping people move away from ego-dystonic behavior and toward ego-syntonic behavior. Yet bullying, for some young people, is an ego-syntonic behavior, or one with which young people are completely comfortable. Bullies often see their actions as justified, even inevitable. They will say: "I hit him *because* he looked at me," "I called him names *because* he's a geek," or "She *deserves it* when I talk about her behind her back because she talked to my boyfriend." These statements reflect bullies' sense of cause and effect. Bullies tell us that they have to harass others who are different or who challenge their authority. In dealing with ego-syntonic behavior, it is important that we avoid assuming that people want to change. When a behavior is ego-syntonic, our job is more complex than when we start out allied with a person's desire to act differently.

If we want to succeed, we must structure situations in which the behavior stops gratifying the desires of bullies and instead becomes costly. A young man whom I saw in therapy some years ago helped me see this issue more clearly. Roger was 14 years old. A young girl told her parents that Roger had sexually molested her while he was baby-sitting. The police found convincing physical evidence that Roger had in fact molested the girl.

> The cost of the bullying behavior for the bully is an important part of the process of change.

Roger's first reaction was to claim that the girl was lying. He showed no guilt and no awareness that the girl could have been hurt by the behavior she described. He was scheduled for trial when I began working with him. During the months leading up to his trial date, I saw him begin to acknowledge that he had indeed molested the girl. Gradually, I saw him begin to realize that she had been frightened and hurt by the experience. However, one day he walked into my office as jaunty and cocky as he had been at the first meeting. The serious, thoughtful demeanor of our recent sessions was gone. When I asked him what had changed, he said, "I realized that whatever I did wasn't such a big deal. Maybe I didn't do anything." I found out from his parents that since the chain of custody of the physical evidence had been broken, the charges against Roger had been dropped. Knowing that his actions were no longer going to cause him any consequences, he did not continue to examine or learn from his behavior.

Many young people and adults, even after hearing the reasons for bullying discussed thus far, still ask me why some young people bully while others do not. It is hard for many of us to understand how anyone could willingly cause pain to another. I add that there are environmental and parenting factors that make it more likely that a young person will bully, some of which I will discuss later when I summarize Dr. Olweus's research. There are also studies linking violent television with aggressive behavior.

| TV and aggression. |

Psychologist L. Rowell Huesmann, who has published a 15-year study of the effects of television on youth (Huesmann et al., 2003), states that violence in television, especially when used by charismatic heroes, shows young people that violence is an appropriate way to deal with some situations. Huesmann writes that violent television erodes young people's natural aversion to violence. His study found that young people who watch more violent television are more likely to abuse spouses as adults and to assault others. He learned that certain television shows have a more profound effect on behavior than others. The shows that affect behavior most profoundly are those in which young people identify with and like the violent character, in which the violent character is praised or rewarded for violence, and which young people describe as realistic. The day after I read this study I met with four kindergarten students who were staying in at recess because they had kicked or punched others. I asked them what their favorite TV show was. They all named the same show: *Walker, Texas Ranger.* This realistically filmed show follows the story of a "good guy" in danger. The hero of the show is threatened by groups of people who wish to kill him. He must beat up the "bad guys," using graphically realistic physical violence to save his own life. At the end of each show, the governor, president, or FBI thanks the "hero" for stopping crime. A closer fit with the Huesmann research would be hard to find.

Another element of young people's electronic environment is video games. Because violent video games are a recent invention, long-term research on their effects has yet to be completed. It is clear from everything we know about human learning that people learn any lesson more deeply through repeated practice than through observation. I believe we should be deeply concerned about the impact that "playing" violent video games has on young people. One excellent resource for educating parents and communities about video games is Lt. Col. David Grossman's segment of the video "Game Over: Gender, Race, and Violence in Video Games." Grossman, a West Point psychology professor, professor of military science, and an Army Ranger, writes in an interview (Grossman, 2000):

> [Military killing simulators] are powerful devices that have great safeguards built into them, in which the goal is to teach under what circumstances you can shoot. . . . The point is, the law-enforcement officer stands up with a FATS [Fire Arms Training Simulator] trainer, and he holds a gun in his hand, he pulls the trigger, the slide slams back, he feels the recoil; if he hits the target on the screen, the target drops; if he misses the target, the target shoots him.
>
> Well, go to the video arcade, and play a game called "Time Crisis." You hold the gun in your hand, you pull the trigger, the slide slams back, you feel the recoil. You hit the target, the target drops. You miss the target, the target shoots you. This is a murder simulator. It is no longer a killing simulator for individuals who, reluctantly, under proper circumstances, we acknowledge, maybe have to kill. It is a device placed in the hands of children, whose only social characteristic is to give him the skill and the will to kill. . . . [W]hen the children play the violent video games, they're drilling, drilling, drilling—not two times a year—every night, to kill every living creature in front of you, until you run out of targets or you run out of bullets . . . [W]e

are drilling these kids to be killers, and to associ-
ate pleasure and reward with it! . . . It is the psychological equivalent of putting an M-16 or a
Glock pistol in the hands of every child in America.

Yet, when we talk about environmental factors in aggression,
we risk ignoring a significant factor that determines who will bully

> Aggression is a choice people make.

and who will not. We need to remember that
young people choose their own behavior. Even
in the face of social modeling, media violence,
and adults' failure to act, most young people
choose not to bully. Our challenge is to hold
those who bully completely accountable for the choices they make
while we also work to change the factors predisposing youth to bully.

William Glasser (1975) writes in *Reality Therapy,* "[In ther-
apy] someone cares enough about the patient to make him face a
truth he has spent his life trying to avoid: he is responsible for his
own behavior" (p. 34). The more we know about the causes of
aggressive behavior, the more we must remind ourselves that we
can help young people change only when we hold them fully responsible for their actions. Decades of education by mental health experts
has formed a society in which we often ask, "What are the issues
in the lives of children that make them act this way?" instead of
asking, "What choices do children make, and how can we help them
make other choices in the future?" More than 30 years as a therapist have taught me that most young people are better served by a
focus on helping them find positive ways to meet their needs than
they are by a search for the causes of their behavior.

Why do some young people become targets of bullying while
others do not? A school where I presented asked its students before
I arrived, "Why are people bullied at our school?" All of the answers
gave characteristics of the target. All 300 students listed weight,
intelligence, appearance, poverty, clumsiness, and many other

"causes" for bullying. As I talked with the students and challenged their answers to this question, they told me that bullies, not targets, cause bullying. Students all over the country tell me that bullies choose targets who they think no one will "stick up for." In some schools, smart kids are seen as outsiders and thus become easy targets for bullies. In other schools, students who are clumsy or unathletic are the outsiders. Bullying is a behavior based on opportunity. Some young people are targeted over others because the bully sees that no one will stand up for them. Then the bully invents reasons that the target "asked for it."

As we see bullying as a choice made by bullies and realize that many bullies are quite comfortable with their behavior, we are ready to begin looking at the effects of bullying and techniques for making schools safer communities.

Suggested Reading

Olweus (1993) and Craig and Pepler (2000a) provide a thorough overview of bullying prevention. Juvonen, Graham, and Schuster (2003) present a detailed look at characteristics of bullies and targets. Shepard's (2004) novel shows us the inner life of a humiliated boy.

The book *RAMPAGE: The Social Roots of School Shootings,* by Katherine Newman (2004), rests on in-depth interviews at the scene of two school shootings and makes clear, research-based recommendations for schools. For all of us who have wondered why these shootings happen and what we can do to prevent them, this book is indispensable. See also Kimmel and Mahler (2003) for another analysis of school shootings.

Over the years, I have become increasingly aware of the importance of addressing gender issues as part of any intervention to stop bullying. Two people whose work has influenced me are Lyn Mikel Brown (2005) and Michael Kimmel (Kimmel & Mahler, 2003).

CHAPTER 2

THE PREVALENCE AND EFFECTS OF BULLYING

In the early 1980s, as part of a major study of childhood pain, we asked children with leukemia what their worst pain experience had been. We expected the answers to be some of the often excruciating treatment-related pains that these children must endure. To our astonishment, many children said that their worst pain was to be teased about their appearance (for example, baldness and extreme pallor) when they returned to school.

—Dorothea Ross (1996)

Almost 11 percent of U.S. students are bullied frequently.

The quote on the previous page reminds us of the devastating impact bullying can have on young people. Before we discuss the effects of bullying in more depth, we will talk about its prevalence. How common is bullying? The numbers vary from study to study. A 2002 American Medical Association study of over 15,000 students found that almost 11 percent of American students in grades 6–10 reported that they were bullied frequently. Thirteen percent reported that they bullied others frequently (Nansel, Overpeck, Pilla et al., 2001; Espelage, 2002). Reading these numbers as percentages may lead us to underestimate the seriousness of the problem. There are, according to the National Center for Education Statistics, almost 50 million students in school in the United States, which means that more than 5 million students in the United States are bullied frequently. Over 6 million more bully consistently. These numbers make bullying the most common form of violence in our society (National Association of School Psychologists, 2002).

Many of us know from our childhood experiences that bullying has long-lasting consequences for targets. Studies have linked bullying to increased rates of childhood and adult depression, suicide, aggression, and lower academic achievement. Children who are bullied are more likely to be lonely and to have difficulty making friends. Baumeister, Twenge, and Nuss (2002) found that peer rejection significantly reduces students' scores on IQ test items and their ability to reason analytically. In a study called "Does Bullying Cause Emotional Problems? A Prospective Study of Young Teenagers," Bond et al. (2001) state that 30 percent of adolescent depression in their survey sample could be attributed to peer harassment. This effect was strongest in girls. Mynard, Joseph, and Alexander's 2000 study, "Peer Victimization and Post-Traumatic Stress in Adolescence," compared the effects of verbal victimization (name-calling) and social manipulation (systematic exclusion) on adolescents. They found that social manipulation predicted symp-

toms of posttraumatic stress, verbal victimization predicted a lower sense of self-worth, and
when young people believe that others control
their lives, they are more likely to have low self-
worth and posttraumatic stress symptoms. As a
student said to me in Missouri, "They say that
sticks and stones can break your bones but words

> Social exclusion is the most damaging form of bullying.

can never hurt you. The way I see it, sticks and stones can break
your bones, and words can break your heart."

Young people have taught me that there are three stages in the
traumatic impact of bullying on targets. The first stage, the bullying itself, is painful. Bullying leads to reduced feelings of safety
and comfort within a target's environment.

At the second stage, targets often see bystanders, who they
thought cared about them, doing nothing to stop the bullying. When
most peers and teachers do not defend targets from bullying, targets begin to feel that those peers and teachers agree with the bully
and support the harassment. A student in Ohio said, "When people
watch you being bullied and do nothing, that makes you believe
that you deserve it." A student in Maine said, "When people bully
you and no one helps, it's like you don't count." A student in San
Diego said, "First they bully you, then you bully yourself." Young
people often tell me that "everyone" picks on them, even when the
active bullying only comes from a few peers.

The third stage in the effect of bullying on young people comes
when targeted youth are excluded from friend-
ships because they are seen as weak or "different." As targets are often perceived as weak and
out of the mainstream, peers often see them as
less desirable friends and tend to avoid them.
Bullies also sometimes pressure peers to exclude
targets from friendship. Afraid of being bullied
themselves, peers often comply.

> When targets of bullying are excluded by peers, bystanders add to the hurt.

I have asked young people at the end of each workshop how they want peers to react if they are bullied. I ask them if they would rather their peers tell the bully to stop, tell adults, or reach out in friendship. Fourth to eighth graders from all across the country choose reaching out in friendship as the most desired peer intervention, often by ratios of ten to one.

Bullies risk growing up as criminals.

Bullying is harmful to bullies as well because bullying is a strong predictor of adult criminality. Dorothea Ross (1996) quotes Eron, Huesmann, Dubow, Romanoff, and Yarnell's longitudinal study showing that

> children who bullied at age 8 had a 1 in 4 chance of ending up with a criminal record by the age of 30, as compared to the 1 in 20 chance that most children have. They were more likely to be convicted of serious crimes . . . and were more abusive to their wives and children. (p. 68)

Dr. Olweus (1993) found similar results when studying middle school bullies. Dake, Price, and Telljohann (2003) found that

> bullies were significantly more likely to become involved in self-destructive behaviors such as alcohol use . . . tobacco use . . . and fighting. . . . Significant relationships also existed with bullying others and weapon carrying, cheating on tests . . . stealing . . . vandalism . . . having trouble with the police, and skipping school. (p. 174)

Connolly, Craig, Pepler, and Taradash (2000) explored the dating experiences of bullies. They found that bullies were significantly more likely than non-bullies to report engaging in physical and social aggression with their boyfriends and girlfriends.

It is not clear to me that being a bully makes a young person more likely to become violent toward dating partners and commit other crimes. It may be that bullying behavior is the first expression of forces in a child's development that, without intervention, will lead to later criminality. It is clear to me that if adult and peer intervention is infrequent, and if bullies experience feelings of power and respect from peers for their actions, it is likely that they will become more aggressive as time goes on. No matter whether bullying is a dependable early indicator of later aggression or part of the cause of later aggression, effective and early intervention can prevent much social harm to others as well as to bullies themselves.

Finally, bullying is harmful to entire school communities. Over the past several years, bullying has gained the spotlight as a possible cause for violent physical assaults, including school shootings. Christine Gregoire, attorney general for the state of Washington, wrote:

> During my tenure as president of the National Association of Attorneys General in 1999–2000, my fellow attorneys general and I visited schools . . . to learn first hand the causes of youth violence. . . . Overwhelmingly, I heard that the causes of youth violence lie first in the home and that the second leading cause of youth violence is the bullying, teasing, harassing, and tormenting that occur in schools. . . . While both students and teachers agreed that bullying was pervasive, most believed that little action had been taken to stop it. (2001)

There are certainly other causes for severe school violence. It is clear, though, that bullying, when not addressed by effective intervention, is a serious matter for targets, bullies, and the health of the entire school community.

Suggested Reading

Dake, Price, and Telljohann's 2003 article; Craig and Pepler (2000a); and Garbarino and DeLara (2002) provide a detailed view of bullying, its incidence, and its effects.

CHAPTER 3

DISCARDING COMMON MYTHS ABOUT BULLYING

Ask adults whether bullying is a problem, and you're bound to get a variety of answers. On one side of the fence, we hear rationalizations for bullying such as, "It happened to me when I was growing up, and I turned out OK"; "It's just part of growing up"; "It's just kids having fun"; and "It's no big deal." On the other side, we hear the harsh reality of how bullying can truly affect children and adolescents. "I hate going to school because of what goes on there," "I think about suicide all the time because of the way I get treated," or, in the words of Eric Harris—one of the Columbine shooters—"This is what you get for the way you treated us."

—William Voors (2003)

Parallels to other forms of abuse and harassment: What have we learned?

It is difficult to change the assumptions about bullying that pervade our culture and impede our progress in bullying prevention. The best way I have found to correct our misconceptions is to look at the myths and attitudes historically surrounding other parallel forms of abuse and to retrace the path we have followed in learning how to reduce these behaviors. As we examine our journey, we find that many abusive behavior patterns were once seen as normal. Cultural beliefs and values that we have now abandoned enabled the abusive behavior to continue. In each case, our society tried a series of ineffective responses to the problem. We have discovered interventions that reduce some of these abusive behaviors. A few examples of these parallel types of harassment include racial discrimination, sexual harassment, and spousal abuse.

These examples share core similarities with childhood bullying. Each form of abuse involves a power differential, with a more powerful group or individual taking advantage of their power over another group or individual. In each case, abusers justify their behavior by placing blame and responsibility on the victims. Additionally, targets in all of these examples may internalize the abuse, thus prolonging and deepening the effects of the harassment and further empowering the aggressors. In each case, there has been a history of silence from bystanders, often leading to targets' sense of isolation. During my lifetime I have seen many different interventions used to solve each of these social problems.

Two of the most important strategies have been efforts to increase public awareness and enforce clear standards through consequences for abusive behavior. These efforts have met with some success, and the work continues.

Let's discuss these historical examples in more detail. Many factors supported racial discrimination—the power of the government, laws that either codified or allowed discrimination, and widely held and rarely challenged cultural assumptions. Those in power took advantage of their power while explaining their actions through pointing to the supposed "inferiority" of people of color. It took a long time for these deep-seated beliefs and assumptions to be challenged by significant numbers of whites. The civil rights movement of the 1960s raised national awareness and made it clear that segregation and racial discrimination in housing, voting, and employment could no longer continue. Finally, it took the will of the people and the power of the federal government to change the institutions of segregation and reduce discrimination. Laws and penalties were needed to make change possible.

Sexual harassment is another example that parallels bullying. Sexual harassment was and is made possible by the power men have in many workplaces and by the power held by employers and supervisors. There was a time, not long ago, when sexual harassment was accepted as a normal part of life, as bullying often is today.

It was not until the mid-1970s that women began to speak out against this form of abuse. Even after targets of sexual harassment and their allies began speaking up, it took years for institutions and laws to hold perpetrators accountable for their behavior. The *Reader's Companion to U.S. Women's History* states about sexual harassment, "Law now exposes this practice of bigotry rather than colluding in silence. [As a result] sexual harassment has become less legitimate and less costly to resist" (Smith, Steinem, & Mink, 1998).

Efforts to prevent sexual harassment have required a focus both on raising awareness and on holding perpetrators accountable for their actions through the judicial system. As definitions of sexually harassing behavior have evolved over time, there has been progress in setting objective and uniform standards and guidelines. Schools and societies go through a parallel process in deciding which behaviors to define and sanction as bullying.

> Changing sexual harassment requires clear definitions and consequences as well as education.

Similarly, spousal abuse has been seen for millennia as a family matter beyond the control of society or courts. Angela Browne (1989) writes that physical domination of wives by husbands has been condoned for centuries. She says that English law, for example, gave husbands authority over their wives, allowing men to beat their wives with whips and clubs. In the United States, it was not until the late nineteenth century that states began to move away from supporting husbands when they used physical force to discipline their wives (Epstein, 1999). Even in the recent past, many people have clung to the opinion that, in the absence of serious violence, the government should not interfere in family matters. Finally, in 1994, the Violence Against Women Act was passed. This law states, "All persons within the United States shall have the right to be free from crimes of violence motivated by gender" (United States Department of Justice, Office on Violence Against Women, 2004). This law preceded others, including mandatory arrest laws and the extension of restraining orders across state lines. While domestic violence is still a serious problem, wider awareness and laws that hold abusers legally responsible have contributed to lower rates of abuse.

In working against racial discrimination, sexual harassment, and domestic violence, our society has followed a similar sequence of reactions to the behavior. First, we denied that the behavior existed, did significant harm, or was intentional. Included in this denial phase were attitudes that rationalized the abusive behavior. As recently as the 1970s, I can remember hearing people explaining domestic violence by saying, "He just doesn't know his own strength," or "Men are like that."

> Blaming the targets of harassment.

Second, we blamed targets by claiming that they provoked the abusive behavior through their own actions or inactions. A woman reporting sexual harassment might have been told, "Look at the blouses you wear!" We advised targets about how to stop the abusive behavior, as though they had the power to make the abuser stop. Targets of domestic violence were advised to avoid spousal abuse by learning to cook better or submit to their husband in order to protect the fragile male ego. There is a significant risk that this advice further solidified beliefs held by targets that they were to blame for the abuse. This intervention does little to change abusive behaviors and nothing to hold abusers responsible for their actions.

The next step we traveled in all these examples of abuse represents a critical shift from holding targets responsible to holding abusers responsible. In this step our society attempted to convince abusers to stop through public information campaigns stressing the negative effects of abusive behavior.

Although these campaigns were well meaning, by themselves these efforts have been largely ineffective because they ignore the reality that many abusers already know that their behavior hurts their targets and choose their actions for that purpose.

Finally, our society has worked for successful change through a combination of strategies. These strategies include clearly defining the behavior to be changed, enforcing rules and

> What has worked?

laws to raise the cost of the behavior to the perpetrator, modeling positive behavior, and changing the widespread acceptance of the behavior. This combination of interventions has been the most effective tool in changing social patterns of abuse.

Our attitudes about bullying follow a similar pattern. First, we may deny that bullying is a problem in our schools. I hear teachers say, "We don't have a bullying problem here," despite student statements to the contrary. We deny that bullying is a serious problem by insisting that it is just a normal part of growing up. Finally, we deny that children we know are bullies by saying that we know they don't mean to hurt anyone.

Parallel ways we blame the targets of bullying.

We blame targets of bullying in several ways. I often hear youth telling me that targets of bullying cause abuse by "not standing up for themselves." We focus on the characteristics of targets that make them different. Teachers and parents tell me, "Linda is teased *because* she is overweight," "Doug is teased *because* he has Asperger's syndrome," or "Carrie is teased *because* she's intellectually gifted." Students also assume that the characteristics of targets cause bullying, as shown by the school survey I mentioned earlier. The survey asked students, "Why are people bullied here?" None of these students initially said that students are bullied because bullies choose to bully them, or because adults and bystanders don't intervene.

I hear from youth that adults are likely to advise targets in ways to stop the bullying themselves. Adults advise targets to stand up for themselves, ignore bullies, learn to make friends, walk away, and not let the bullying bother them because bullies are "just jealous anyhow" or "don't mean it." These interventions are common, well meaning, and often ineffective, for reasons I have already discussed.

Many schools attempt to teach respect and caring through presentations and activities that encourage students to recognize the effects of their cruel actions on others. Although these are productive activities for many students, bullies are unlikely to listen to or care about these lessons unless the lessons are backed up by rules and consequences that increase the costs of their aggressive actions.

Finally, in the step that I have seen make the difference, we combine clear definitions of the behavior to be changed with the consistent enforcement of standards. While holding bullies responsible for their actions, we commend them for their positive actions, model positive behaviors, and work to implement a schoolwide change in culture.

Parallels between racial discrimination, sexual harassment, domestic violence, and bullying can help us choose interventions. For all of these forms of harassment, we have moved from seeing abusive behaviors as normal and provoked by targets to holding abusers responsible for their bad choices. We have moved from considering these behaviors as inevitable to seeing them as unacceptable. Behavior previously seen as a private matter is now recognized as affecting society as a whole. Finally, greater awareness leads to the enforcement of laws and rules, which show abusers that their behaviors are unacceptable and lead to consequences and which empower targets of harassment.

I encourage you to think about the advice you give targets of bullying and ask if you would give the same advice to targets of sexual harassment, racial discrimination, or spousal abuse. Would we tell a woman experiencing sexual harassment to "Pretend it doesn't bother you"? Would we tell someone being abused by a spouse to "Tell them you don't like what they're doing"? Would we tell a target of discrimination that "Sticks and stones may break your bones, but words will never hurt you"? We can learn from historical struggles for justice.

> We can use these analogies to help us think about the advice we give to targets of bullying.

Suggested Reading

Ross (1996) presents many of the myths and realities about bullying. Wessler (2003) presents the consequences of ignoring low-level harassment. Baumeister's research, especially that of Baumeister, Bushman, and Campbell (2000), addresses common misconceptions about links between self-esteem and aggression.

CHAPTER 4

WHAT DOESN'T WORK?

Seventy-one percent of students report that teachers or other adults in the classroom ignored bullying incidents. When asked, students uniformly expressed the desire that teachers intervene rather than ignore teasing and bullying.

—Christine Gregoire (2001)

Before we discuss in greater detail what works to prevent bullying, let us examine what many adults currently do, or fail to do, that
is likely to make things worse. Before discussing bullying prevention
interventions that are unlikely to work, I feel I should repeat some-

> I have
> personally
> made all the
> mistakes I will
> be discussing
> here.

thing I said in the introduction. *I have made all of
the mistakes I will talk about in this book—some
of them many times.* As I criticize interventions, I
am not criticizing the good people who carry out
these interventions. Instead, I am providing this
information in the hope that people will use their
limited time and energy in directions that are likely
to be effective. I also want to stress that some of
the interventions I will discuss here, while unlikely to be effective
alone, can be effective within the context of a systematic intervention.

Although many teachers assume that they are aware of the amount
of bullying in their schools, Wendy Craig and Debra Pepler (2000a)
found the opposite to be true. Craig and Pepler, Canadian researchers
who have spent their careers studying bullying in schools, planted
hidden cameras and microphones in elementary school playgrounds
and classrooms. They watched and listened to the tapes in order to
identify the prevalence of bullying and the extent of adult intervention. They found an average of one incident of bullying every seven
minutes. They found that adults intervened in only 4 percent of playground incidents and 14 percent of classroom incidents. When interviewing students and teachers, Craig and Pepler found, despite their
observations, that 71 percent of teachers in those same schools said
that staff almost always intervene in cases of bullying.

The National School Safety Center report on school violence (2001)
found similar patterns in secondary schools in the United States. The
report states that two thirds of 14- to 17-year-olds surveyed said there
is a group of students at their schools who consistently intimidate others while receiving few consequences. Only one third of students surveyed reported that their school penalizes these intimidating students;
less than a third said they report bullying behavior to school staff.

How do we explain this low level of adult intervention? Let me address this question by sharing one of my own experiences working in schools. For my first job as a guidance counselor, I worked at a large K–8 school. Being new, I was assigned to the duty no one else wanted, seventh- and eighth-grade recess duty. Some of the playground rules were harder to enforce than others, with the one banning snowballs an especially tough one for me.

I approached the principal to ask her about the rule. "Throwing snowballs is fun," I said, "and who gets hurt?" The principal patiently explained to me that throwing snowballs always leads to throwing ice balls and then rocks, and that someone inevitably gets hurt. It is best to stop the behavior early, she said, a principle I have since found to be a crucial element of successful violence prevention.

Even after I understood the reasons behind the rule, I still encountered difficulties enforcing it. The playground was large, and it was hard to see everything at once. When I did catch students throwing snowballs and approached them with my clipboard, the most common response was, "Mrs. Brown never writes us up for snowballs. Mr. Walker lets us throw snowballs. What's wrong with YOU?" I realized that these students, instead of trying to manipulate me, were telling the truth. I was the only person enforcing the rule. I gradually stopped enforcing it.

In my experience, rules are enforced inconsistently for three reasons. First, teachers may not discuss with each other what rules are important to them and why. Sometimes rules are part of a purchased discipline system or are created unilaterally by the principal or the school board. In these cases, school staff often do not see the point of some of the rules and so enforce only those that they care about. Over time, inconsistency causes even lower levels of enforcement,

> Staff inconsistency in enforcing rules makes rules harder to enforce, even by people who believe in them.

as students challenge staff the way the students on the playground challenged me.

| If rules are difficult to enforce, there will be inconsistency. |

The second reason for inconsistent administration of rules involves the amount of time involved in enforcing rules. When already overburdened staff members who observe negative behavior are expected to sacrifice significant amounts of teaching or preparation time to follow through with consequences, they are less likely to enforce rules. It becomes easier to ignore behavior than to stop oneself from being able to teach.

| Vague rules will not be enforced. |

The third reason for inconsistent enforcement of rules has to do with the specificity of the rules themselves. When rules are poorly defined, enforcement is more likely to be inconsistent. Rules like "We will respect each other and be kind" are hard to enforce. This sentence is an effective statement of principle but a vague behavioral expectation. Fifty different staff members will interpret this rule in 50 different ways, leading to inconsistent enforcement.

| Inconsistency teaches bullies that their behavior is OK. It teaches targets that they deserve to be bullied. |

What does inconsistent, and therefore infrequent, adult intervention tell bullies? What does it tell targets? Our inaction tells bullies that their behavior is acceptable. Instead of learning to control or change their behavior, youth learn that consequences are arbitrary and dependent on the mood of whatever adult is watching them. When bullies get in trouble only once out of 25 times, and when some students get in trouble for the same behaviors that others display freely, all students learn that life is unfair and that the problem does not lie in the behavior of students. Targets learn that change is unlikely and that they are helpless to make changes.

The story of one young man with whom I worked helped me see how our most common reactions to bullying can do more harm than good. Peter attended the elementary school where I work, then moved to a middle school in a nearby school district. Peter experienced frequent harassment from a group of boys at his new school for a year and a half before his parents finally called me to ask for advice. The bullies stopped him in the hall and made insinuating comments implying that Peter was homosexual. They made fun of his way of talking and walking. They stroked his cheek and made fun of his awkward, overwhelmed reactions to their behavior. At first, Peter was too embarrassed to tell his parents. When he did tell his parents about the harassment, they told him to talk to the principal. He finally talked to the principal, and the principal yelled at Peter, telling him that the school couldn't help if Peter didn't report the behavior right away. When Peter went home, he told his parents that he felt intimidated and blamed for the harassment. Peter refused to talk to the principal again.

Next, Peter's parents suggested that Peter talk to the school counselor, who told him to tell the boys that their behavior bothered him. Peter did tell the boys, who then began teasing him for being a baby who was unable to take a joke. Peter returned to the counselor, who set up a meeting with all parties involved. After that, the boys began teasing him for running to an adult for help.

Peter talked to his physical education teacher, who suggested that Peter pretend that the bullies' behavior did not bother him. Peter experienced two problems in using this strategy. First, Peter did not have the level of acting training necessary to convince the boys that he didn't mind what they were doing. Second, the boys reacted to his efforts by trying harder to get a reaction from Peter. At this point it was clear that each adult intervention left Peter worse

off—more isolated, with fewer people to appeal to, and experiencing more frequent harassment.

As I discuss this series of incidents with thousands of teachers
in training workshops, they tell me that all the strategies suggested
by the adults in Peter's life are common practice in adult reactions
to bullying. They also agree that none of these approaches is likely
to work. Why then, I ask each group, do teachers continue to attempt
these interventions? They tell me that educators have little else they
can do when there is no schoolwide intervention and that educators don't know what else to do.

Many of us are bound by myths about bullying. We have been
told that we should not intervene because by intervening we will
encourage further harassment and weaken the target.

Often we have been led to believe, as I was, that bullying is a
normal and inevitable part of growing up. We hope that resilient
children will get over name-calling and other verbal bullying by
themselves. Many of us have been taught that punishing bullies
hurts their already weakened self-esteem and causes them to behave
more aggressively.

I will write later about what *did* work with Peter. Let's start for
now with one key idea: Much of what we do to help targets of bullying actually makes the bullying worse. Based on bullying prevention research and my own mistakes, I have found the following
interventions, when used alone and not as part of a comprehensive
intervention, unlikely to have much long-term effect.

Speaking to students at large about the importance of kindness
and charity, without any systemic disciplinary action for cruelty, is
unlikely to have much effect on aggressive youth. I have received
many letters from students telling me, "They talk about bullying
every year and nothing ever changes." "Teachers yell at the bullies

and then no one does anything." The majority of students are already kind to each other, and the students who do bully don't listen during presentations promoting kindness and charity. When I used to lead these kinds of workshops, teachers would tell me afterwards, "It was a good presentation. It was too bad that the students who needed to hear it weren't listening." Students who bully consistently already know that their actions cause distress to targets. Telling them that words hurt is unlikely to change their behavior.

Similarly, peer mediation is unlikely to be effective against harassment, which is not conflict between equal-status peers. Mediators, especially those without substantial training and personal maturity, are likely to help bullies solidify their position of power over targets. Peer mediation programs are especially unlikely to work when implemented alone instead of as a part of broader attempts to improve discipline (Sherman et al., 1997).

Bystander training can have some effect in the absence of a comprehensive program, but is unlikely to make significant long-lasting change unless staff members actively model the behaviors they are trying to encourage and protect bystanders. Here I see a parallel to neighborhood watch programs, which can only be successful if police response is swift and effective and if people reporting crimes are protected from retaliation by criminals.

Training for targets, as a stand-alone intervention, is no more likely to end bullying than it would be likely to end sexual harassment or spousal abuse. In our society's reaction to bullying, there has been a significant focus on bully-proofing children so they cannot be teased or humiliated. Most popular literature and films about bullying show targets finally standing up for themselves and solving their problems alone.

> Training for targets is unlikely to work except as part of a schoolwide program.

The reality is that bullies rarely listen to their targets. When we train youth to stand up for themselves and do not also stand up for them ourselves, we risk leaving them feeling more isolated and hopeless if their actions do not work.

We adults should also rethink the everyday ways in which we make bullying more likely. Here are a few examples. I encourage you to look for others.

First, the word *tattling* and the negative connotations that accompany it discourage young people from reporting harassment. I know that young people sometimes do come to teachers with trivial concerns. They do need to learn to solve some of their own problems. We need to remember, though, that they often do need our help. Dorothea Ross (1996) found in her research that most targets of bullying tried many other interventions before asking adults for help. If we show targets verbally and nonverbally that we are annoyed by their requests for help, they are likely to suffer in silence in the future. Speaking up about injustice is a good thing. It is our job as adults to encourage youth to continue to do so.

Asking students to choose their own teams and groups gives students an easy way to exclude and harass slow, clumsy, and socially awkward students by choosing them last and making critical comments about them. It is easier and less painful for the less popular students if we assign groups randomly.

Additionally, leaving young people unsupervised allows harassment to take place. When we ask students where harassment is likely to happen, they tell us that high-risk places include playgrounds, buses, halls, locker rooms, and lunchrooms.

Even more important, the attitudes and opinions of staff members have a profound impact on students. Adults who consider teasing a natural consequence of obnoxious or "different" behavior will make bullying more likely. I have often heard the following types of comments from teachers: "She asked for the harassment," "He smells bad and so they tease him," or "He gets bullied because he has no social skills." Our cultural conditioning tells us that unusual people will be teased and physically harassed. If we are not careful, we will fail to attribute responsibility for that harassment to the bullies themselves. In a democratic society, it is our job as adults to support young people's rights to be safe, even if they are socially awkward, physically clumsy, or otherwise different, just as it is our job to protect young people from harassment based on religion, race, or gender. We need to remember that it is not inevitable that differences will lead to bullying.

The most fundamental ways adults make bullying more likely are the most subtle. When adults show that we value some students over others, that we dislike some students, and that we treat some students with disrespect, we model these behaviors for our students. When we realize what kind of behavior we are modeling, we can make fundamental changes.

As an example of this principle, I will tell the story of a fifth-grade teacher who asked for my help in stopping the harassment in his classroom. He told me that his students were harassing a girl named Cindy, who was moderately mentally retarded and came from a primitive home environment. She had rudimentary social skills and sometimes smelled bad. When she spoke in class, other students laughed at her. Students argued about being forced to work with her and called her names.

We planned a time for me to come in and talk to the whole class, but the teacher and I were both busy and weeks passed. I met the teacher in the hall one day and asked when would be a good time for me to meet with his students. He smiled sheepishly and told me that he had solved the problem. I asked for more details.

A deeply religious man, the teacher told me that he had prayed about the problem and, as a result, started to examine his own behavior toward Cindy. As he watched himself interact with her, he noticed that he himself ignored her questions, was often impatient with her, and criticized her actions in front of her peers. When he started treating Cindy with more respect, he found that his students also changed their behavior.

> When we show by our actions that we value every student, we encourage our students to do the same.

There are many ways that teachers can reduce bullying. When we stop our behaviors that make the problem worse, we take the first step. When we clarify expectations and make sure that students experience effective consequences for aggression toward peers, we reduce the frequency of bullying. Most important, when we show by our actions and our positive attention that we value every student, we encourage our students to do the same.

Suggested Reading

Garbarino and DeLara (2002) present the words of many teens who ask that adults be more active in stopping harassment. Perlstein (2003) shows us that just teaching strategies for coping with bullying or telling young people not to let bullying bother them isn't enough.

CHAPTER 5

THE OLWEUS RESEARCH

The [Olweus bullying prevention] program strives to develop a school (and ideally, a home) environment:
- *characterized by warmth, positive interest, and involvement by adults;*
- *firm limits to unacceptable behavior;*
- *where non-hostile, nonphysical negative consequences are consistently applied in cases of violations of rules and other unacceptable behaviors; and,*
- *where adults act as authorities and positive role models.*

—Daniel Olweus, Susan Limber,
and Sharon Mihalic (1997)

In 1982, three Norwegian boys ages 10–14 committed suicide, apparently as a result of severe bullying by their classmates. The event triggered shock and outrage, led to a national campaign against bullying behavior, and resulted in the development of a systematic school-based bullying intervention program. The psychologist Dan Olweus developed the intervention program and tested it on more than 2,500 students in Bergen, Norway. After two years, incidents of school bullying dropped by more than 50 percent. Since then, a number of countries, including England, Germany, and the United States, have implemented Olweus's program, with 30–70 percent reductions in bullying (Starr, 2000). Dr. Olweus has continued to develop and research his intervention and now supervises its replication in countries around the globe.

Dr. Olweus began his research by looking at family characteristics that make bullying more likely. He found that bullies often come from families where parents spend little time with their children and where discipline is inconsistent and episodic. His findings mirror other research that identifies spending time nurturing youth, maintaining a positive tone, and ensuring disciplinary consistency as highly significant in predicting outcomes for children. Olweus's description of parenting styles also parallels Diane Baumrind's 1966 and 1967 work identifying three types of parenting.

Styles of parenting.

Baumrind proposed a distinction between authoritative, authoritarian, and permissive parents. Authoritative parents set limits while accepting their children's uniqueness and feelings. As their children grow, they give them increasing autonomy while maintaining clear limits and consistent consequences. Authoritarian parents impose their will in arbitrary, strict ways and allow children little autonomy or flexibility. Permissive parents nurture but impose few limits. Dumas and Nilsen (2003), summarizing research that has been done about authoritative parenting, report that parents who are authoritative have adolescents who are better adjusted and more competent than their peers with authoritarian or permissive parents. The [teens] are confident in their abilities, competent in many different areas, and unlikely to have psychological difficulties or to get in trouble for school or conduct problems. (p. 41)

See also Baumrind (1996) for an extensive review of research on these parenting styles and outcomes for youth.

In homes where parents spend time playing with, talking with, and nurturing their children, children learn empathy and social skills. They learn to enjoy cooperative, playful interaction with others. They learn to be kind and nurturing. In homes where little time is spent with children, children learn to seek attention and a sense of belonging in any way they can—sometimes through angering others or through misbehavior.

Effects of parental attention on child development.

In homes where behavioral expectations and disciplinary interventions are consistent and predictable, children learn to control their actions. They learn that their actions lead to positive and negative consequences, that following rules and meeting social expectations lead to better outcomes, and that self-control has benefits. In homes where discipline is inconsistent and unpredictable, children learn that getting what they want depends on the moods of the adults rather than on their own behavior. They learn to manipulate adults, to play one person against another, and to blame adults when things don't go their way. In addition, if harsh or abusive consequences are used in discipline, young people learn that it is legitimate to hurt others to get their way.

Effects of disciplinary consistency on child development.

Olweus built his bullying prevention intervention by structuring school environments that *inverted* the home characteristics that make bullying more likely, creating school environments where adults spend time interacting positively with students and use consistent discipline.

The Olweus bullying intervention includes several components. Schools conduct a student survey to identify rates of bullying, locations where bullying is likely to occur, and how staff members currently react to bullying. Schools implement teacher training and discussion groups to make sure all staff members are grounded in effective intervention.

Schools use the data from the survey to implement supervision during high-risk times. Schools develop specific rules and consistent and immediate consequences for aggressive behavior. The program includes generous praise for prosocial behavior, regular class meetings, and serious talks with bullies and their parents.

I have summarized the Olweus interventions, as I understand them, in the visual on page 49. I have included one theme not directly addressed in the current discussion, but found in Olweus's work. This concept is that of empowering bystanders.

It is important to see the bottom tier of this house diagram as the foundation of our work. As with a house, the foundation underlies the rest of the structure. Without clear, schoolwide definitions of unacceptable behavior and consistently enforced consequences for actions that hurt others, our educational interventions risk failure. Without positive modeling of respectful behavior by adults, lasting change is unlikely. In any effort to change young people's behavior or help them overcome obstacles in their lives, the time we spend with them in nurturing relationships is our most effective tool. The upper tier of this diagram lists interventions that can be effective once that foundation is in place. Once we make it clear that adults will model respectful behavior and hold bullies respon-

```
                          /\
                         /  \
                        /    \
                   Bullying Prevention
        _____
       |              |              |              |
       | Help         | Support      | Empower      |
       | aggressive   | targets      | bystanders   |
       | youth        |              |              |
       | change       |              |              |
       |              |              |              |
       |_____|_____|_____|
       |                                            |
       |     Safe and Affirming School Climate       |
       |_____|
       | Consequences | Positive     | Staff spend   |
       | for aggression:| feedback to | time with     |
       | • inevitable | students;    | students,     |
       | • predictable| positive feeling| especially |
       | • escalating | tone         | students      |
       |              |              | at risk       |
       |_____|_____|_____|
```

sible for their actions, we can work to help bullies develop empathy, support targets in meaningful ways, and empower bystanders to take a stand against bullies.

The rest of this book will discuss the details of implementing the six interventions outlined in this diagram. I will begin by discussing specific interventions to increase positive feedback to students and to build positive staff–student relationships. Then I will focus on building effective discipline systems. After discussing the bottom half of the diagram, I will discuss ways to help bullies change, support targets, empower bystanders, and implement whole-school educational approaches.

My hope in developing the techniques described in this book is to help schools implement Dr. Olweus's research. My work is an expression of my gratitude to him for showing so many of us that we can stop bullying.

Suggested Reading

All of Dr. Olweus's materials are clear and useful. Sharp and Smith (1994) also present important implementation and program details. The U.S. Department of Health and Human Services (2003) publishes a brochure that clearly presents the essentials of the Olweus approach.

CHAPTER 6

ACKNOWLEDGING POSITIVE BEHAVIOR

In my view, there is nothing wrong with helping students and others to take pride in accomplishments and good deeds. But there is plenty of reason to worry about encouraging people to think highly of themselves when they haven't earned it. Praise should be tied to performance (including improvement) rather than dispensed freely as if everyone had a right to it simply for being oneself.

—Roy Baumeister (2001)

> Praise can
> have positive
> or negative
> effects.

Praise is important. It strengthens our relation-ships with students, encourages them to keep trying, and helps them to see what we expect. How we praise is even more important. Although we can all think of praise that has encouraged us, most of us have also had the uncomfortable experience of being praised insincerely or by some-one we didn't trust. We have all seen that praising students may lead to improvement, or it may backfire if they don't believe the truth of what we are saying or don't want their peers to think they are pleasing adults. Dr. Baumeister, in the study quoted at the begin-ning of this chapter, outlines the growing consensus among researchers that praise can either empower youth and support pos-itive change or interfere with growth. In this chapter I will present techniques for effective praise. These techniques help us avoid the risks of controlling or unearned praise. Controlling praise tells young people, "Do this to please me." Unearned praise tells stu-dents they are great without telling them what they have done. Earned praise shows students specifically what they have done and the positive effects of their actions.

> Effective praise
> is descriptive.

There is much research that supports the idea that descriptive praise is more effective than non-descriptive praise in changing behavior (Filcheck, McNeil, & Herschell, 2001; Sutherland, Wehby, & Copeland, 2000). Yet descriptive praise comes in many varieties. Let's begin by thinking about what results we want our praise to have.

We will compare different types of praise by thinking about self-talk, which is how people describe themselves. I agree with Henry Ford when he said, "Whether you think you can or whether you think you can't, you're right." Ford, the psychologist Albert Ellis, and a generation of cognitive-behavioral therapists all tell us that what we believe about ourselves influences how we feel and what we do. Self-talk is important. We tell ourselves that we can accomplish great things if we try, or we tell ourselves that we will fail anyway, so we needn't bother trying.

Think about how the following self-statements influence a student's actions: "I'm dumb," "I'm clumsy," "I'm no good," "I'm lazy," and "I'm immature." When I ask audiences of educators this question, they tell me that these self-statements become self-fulfilling prophecies.

> How do negative self-statements affect behavior?

Students who feel stupid stop trying, students who feel clumsy don't exercise, and students who see themselves as immature use that belief to justify immature behavior. Students who tell themselves that they are stupid, lazy, clumsy, or immature often act in ways that make these statements come true.

Where do these negative self-statements come from? There are many sources for these beliefs, but we cannot deny that they come mostly from adults' statements. Adults tell young people they are lazy. Adults tell young people they are immature. A participant at a recent workshop in New Jersey told me that she heard a colleague say to a student just returning from suspension, "We had such a quiet, peaceful day without you." When we tell young people that they are no good, they may believe us.

Now think about the following self-statements and compare them to the previous statements. What effects do you think these statements have on the behavior of students? "Mom is always mad at me because I don't do my homework," "My teacher doesn't like me because I make noise in class," and "The principal doesn't want me here because I'm always in trouble." Educators in my workshops tell me that these self-statements can affect behavior in two ways: Young people will try harder to obtain adult approval, or they will angrily refuse to seek that approval. Either way, they see their relationships with adults as conditional. Deci and Flaste (1996), in *Why We Do What We Do,* call this the choice between compliance and defiance. Whichever of these paths students choose, they are

Compliance or defiance?

working to meet or defy the expectations of others rather than working to meet internal goals. In addition, when we use negative I-messages such as "I am so disappointed when you hit," we assume that our relationships with students are so strong that they will work hard to change our disappointment. Sometimes the opposite is true.

Here is a third type of negative self-statement: "I got in trouble because I hit," "I did badly on the test because I didn't study," "I couldn't go to the movies because I didn't clean my room." Though these statements describe negative choices, they focus on cause-and-effect relationships rather than negative traits or the negative feelings of adults. They help young people see the connection between their behavior and what happens to them, and thus give them a chance to change.

Calm, descriptive feedback statements that do not include judgments or our feelings are most likely to help youth focus on their own actions and the results of those actions. "You can't go to the movies because you didn't clean your room." "You are inside at recess today because you hit."

Let's think about different types of positive self-statements. Look at this first list and think about what effects these self-statements are likely to have on behavior. "I am smart," "I am kind," "I am great," "I am special," and "I am mature." When I ask educators about the impact of these self-statements on behavior, answers are mixed. At first I hear that students with these beliefs will try harder. Then I hear about students who "know they are smart" and don't try, or students who describe themselves as kind even though they hurt others. A music teacher at a recent workshop told me, "When you tell kids they're talented, they stop practicing." We meet youth who feel entitled because of their perceived superiority. Educators focus on traits rather than behavior at work in another way when meeting parents who teach their children this way of looking at the world. These parents acknowledge that their children hit, tease, and harass others, then go on to say, "He doesn't mean it. He's really a good person."

These parental statements remind me of the time I was visiting a family I was counseling. Their German shepherd clamped his teeth on my knee and began pulling painfully on my kneecap. Wanting their help, I yelled, "Your dog's biting me." They said, "He doesn't mean anything by it," seeming to think that they had solved the problem. I disconnected the dog's mouth from my leg and left.

I think the question to be answered when looking at trait-based self-statements is this: What is the source of students' positive beliefs about themselves? If young people hear about and observe their own accomplishments and positive efforts, they can conclude that they are

> Positive self-statements are helpful if they are earned.

competent, kind, or brave. These earned self-statements help them persist and overcome obstacles. Unearned or unrealistic positive self-statements can lead instead to complacency and a sense of entitlement.

For some youth, unearned positive self-statements can even lead to violent behavior. I quoted Roy Baumeister's research at the beginning of this chapter. The author found that prison inmates with a history of violent crime often describe themselves in unrealistically positive terms. They react violently when others do not recognize their superiority and treat them accordingly. His study found that narcissism—the belief that only one's own feelings and needs matter—was the major difference between violent inmates and nonviolent adults. Baumeister (2001) wrote:

> On narcissism, however, the violent offenders had a
> higher mean score than any other published sample.
> [Narcissism] was the crucial trait that distinguished

these prisoners from college students. . . . Narcissists are no more aggressive than anyone else, as long as no one insults or criticizes them. But when they receive an insult—which could be a seemingly minor remark or act that would not bother other people—the response tends to be much more aggressive than normal. (p. 101)

Now look at the following list of positive self-statements. How are these different? How do you think these self-statements will affect behavior? "Mom loves me because I work hard," "My teacher likes me because I am kind," and "The principal is happy with me because I stay out of trouble." These statements offer young people the choice between compliance and defiance. Often young people choose compliance during childhood and defiance during adolescence. Either way, students are trained to base their opinions of themselves on the people around them. A workshop participant in Atlanta pointed out that I-messages train youth to be codependent and to be controlled by others' feelings.

> **Self-statements that empower.**

Finally, look at one last collection of self-statements. What effects do you think these statements will have on the behavior of young people? "When I work hard, I learn," "When I help others, I feel pride and they are happy," "When I control myself, I stay out of trouble," and "When I play with others, I have a good time." Educators and parents in my training workshops are unanimous in their conclusions that this category of self-statements empowers young people to make autonomous positive choices. This type of cause-and-effect self-statement is at the core of true internal motivation.

What types of praise encourage this last group of self-statements, characterized by feelings of autonomy, responsibility, and cause-and-effect thinking? As I see it, the most effective form of praise incorporates specific observable language. We might say, "I saw Jeremy point his finger at you. Then you walked away." When we acknowledge positive behavior, we act like a video camera, helping students see their own positive actions. We provide a concrete description of what we notice. We stop before the phrases "I'm proud of you" or "Good for you" come out of our mouths by habit.

> Act like a video camera, helping young people see their own positive actions and the effects those actions have.

Here is one example. Last year, in visiting a sixth-grade classroom, I saw a math lesson in which every child got right to work and practiced until the end of the class. I knew that the students didn't know me and it could be risky to tell them they were doing good work, yet I wanted to acknowledge their behavior. I said, "I saw that every one of you got to work right away and worked through the whole class." One of the students said, without any sarcasm, "We must be really special."

Let's discard the endless lists of ways to praise a child. An Internet search on Google found over 800 lists of this type. Almost all of them consisted of vague, meaningless, unearned statements. Here are the beginning phrases from one such list: "wow, neat, good, great, bravo, super, A+ job, awesome, radical, terrific, perfect, how nice, dynamite, good job, good stuff." As I say in my workshops, walking around a classroom talking like this is better than walking around saying, "Stupid, no brains, drop out now, don't bother. . . ." It's just not *much* better. Praise that is vague and unearned does little to encourage students to work hard or take pride in their own actions. At best, they ignore what we say. At worst, they either develop an unearned sense of entitlement or focus on our approval rather than on their own goals for learning. None of these nonspecific statements tells young people what they did that is notable or what kind of effect their behavior will have on themselves and others.

We can also praise through I-messages. We might say, "I'm so happy that you are listening this morning," "I am proud that you are learning," or "I'm glad you worked hard." I-messages are an important tool in conflict resolution and in assertiveness training. I-messages do allow us to discuss relational conflicts in effective ways. Yet, for an I-message to be effective, young people must care about making the adult happy. Many youth at risk have learned not to care about the happiness of the adults in their lives. They may have formed and lost many adult attachments or been subjected to troubled adults who blamed them for their own unhappy feelings. They may have weak attachments with adults and find adults' feelings unimportant.

After I talk about the limitations of I-messages in my teacher workshops, there is almost always discussion about the number of experts who tell educators to use this method of communication. A teacher in Detroit said, "We just went to a workshop where we were taught to tell students how we feel about their behavior. Would you people just agree on one message?" Dr. Jane Bluestein (2003) wrote a clear and insightful article about this topic called "What's Wrong with I-messages?" which focuses on the negative impact of telling others that they are responsible for how we feel.

> Some I-messages tell other people that they are responsible for how we feel.

Dr. Bluestein explains that there are two distinctly different types of I-messages. There are statements that tell others what we are willing or unwilling to do, and there are statements that tell others that they are responsible for our feelings. She focuses on the concept I described previously: that young people should change their behavior for intrinsic reasons whenever possible. She also writes that we are better off telling young people whose friends are cruel to them to say, "I won't play with you if you keep calling me names," rather than "I feel sad when you call me names." The first kind of I-message, which expresses what the speaker is willing or unwilling to do, keeps the speaker in a powerful position. The second type of I-message leaves the speaker in a vulnerable position because the bully can easily say, "Who cares how you feel?" As for parents or teachers, she suggests that we say, "I will listen to you when you talk with me in a calm voice," rather than "I am so hurt when you yell at me."

She writes:

> At first glance, I-messages may seem preferable to You-messages, but in the end, "When you . . . I feel . . ." is a statement of blame. One of the arguments in favor of I-messages that are structured this way is that this formula can help people identify and express their feelings. This may be true, but at what cost? Can't we learn to express our feelings (and teach kids to do the same) without making other people responsible for them? "When you . . . I feel . . ." is, essentially, a form of Victim Talk. It's simply a way to say, "You have the power to create my feelings (and power over my well-being) and I want you to change how you're acting so I don't feel uncomfortable any more." (p. 3)

When targets of bullying tell young people who bully them how they feel about the bullying, they risk giving the bully more control over them. After I described this risk at a workshop in 2005, a counselor e-mailed me to say, "I am an elementary school counselor and wanted to tell you my I-message story":

> A third-grade boy I was working with told me he had tried an I-message with his bullier. "Great!" I said. "What did you say?" He said, "I told him I feel sad and angry when you call me a shrimp every day, and I want you to stop." "Great!" I said. "That was just as we had practiced in class. What happened?" He said, "He gave me an I-message back.

He said, "I don't care!" See, it never works. Nothing will work."

This was the first time I realized [she wrote] that the I-messages that I was teaching the students only worked with two parties who actually care about each other's feelings. I am now implementing an action I-message, such as "I will/will not _____ when you _____," into the elementary guidance curriculum.

> Young people at risk need unconditional, not conditional, love from us.

Another concern people express at workshops is that young people need to hear positive I-messages from adults because many of our most at-risk youth get very little love in their lives and need to know that we care about them. As Kohn (1999) points out, what matters in praise is whether our statements are genuine and whether our nonverbal behavior expresses warmth and concern. He goes on to point out that while at-risk students do need love, they need unconditional love rather than the conditional love that tells them that we only care about them when they do their work or behave. Rather than hearing "I am so happy when you control yourself," they need to see that we choose to spend time with them and that we light up when they come into the room. Then they are able to hear clear behavioral feedback about their positive and negative behavior.

A teacher in Detroit e-mailed me that he had found a way for his eighth-grade students to help him shift from I-messages to descriptive feedback. He told them: "Whenever I tell you that I am happy that you have done your work or disappointed that you haven't, I want you to tell me: 'Yes, Mr. K. It IS all about you.'"

We praise children most effectively by telling them what we observe. We can say to them, "You stayed calm when Tom was yelling at you," "You worked on that project until it was done," "You told the truth," or "You invited Sally to sit with you when she was alone." This form of praise, by showing young people what they did right and what positive impacts their behavior has, encourages them to be proud of their actions. They continue the positive behavior because of this pride. They feel

> We praise children most effectively by telling them what we observe.

a positive sense of control over their own lives. This feedback is especially important for youth with entrenched behavior problems. They often feel a sense of helplessness and lose sight of the ways they can act to make their lives better. When we point out their positive actions and the results of those actions, we help them make more productive choices in the future.

What about mixing these models and including the judgment words like *good, terrific,* or *awesome* in these descriptive statements? The problem with this is that young people's auditory memories are brief. The fewer words in a statement made to them, the more likely it is they will remember the words we want them to remember. "You got right to work and finished your assignment. That means you'll have less homework" is shorter and easier to remember than "That's great! You got right to work and did a wonderful job on your assignment. Look at the terrific way you got it all done. Won't you be happy when you have less homework? Super!" Our time is limited. When we cut to the chase and make our sentences shorter, we can provide effective positive feedback more often.

A similar perspective on the use of feedback comes from the work of Carol Dweck (2000) and Mueller and Dweck (1998). In research spanning 30 years, they studied the effects of what they call "personal praise" and "personal criticism." Personal praise is focused on the child's traits or on an adult's feelings and

> Effects of person-based versus action-based praise or criticism.

includes phrases such as "You're smart," "You're good at this," and "I'm very proud of you." Personal criticism has the same focus and includes phrases such as "You're not good at this" and "I'm disappointed in you." Dweck found that students of all ages react to person-based praise or person-based criticism by avoiding difficult tasks and fearing failure, a pattern she calls helplessness under stress.

She writes that young people who develop helplessness of this kind have great difficulty overcoming challenges and disappointments. When we tell children they are smart, or when we tell them they are stupid, we teach them to judge themselves by the quality of their work. When they have difficulty learning something, they conclude that they are stupid and stop trying. She contrasts the effects of person-based feedback with those of mastery-based feedback such as "You tried hard," "You found a good way to do it. Can you think of another way that would work?" and "The table is still messy. Maybe you should think of another way to get it cleaned up." She found that mastery-based feedback, which focuses on the actions and strategies students use rather than on their traits, leads students to work harder and learn to overcome obstacles rather than to give up in the face of difficulty. Dweck (2000) writes:

> The group that received the person-oriented criticism showed the strongest helpless reaction. . . . Criticism that reflected on the child as a whole created [a] helpless pattern of self-blame, negative affect, and a lack of constructive solutions. . . . Critical feedback that focused the child on alternative strategies produced the most mastery-oriented pattern. (pp. 110–111)

The same pattern applies with praise:

> The groups that had received the most person-oriented praise showed the most . . . helpless pat-

tern. In contrast, the groups that had gotten the effort and strategy praise looked the most mastery-oriented. . . . Person criticism and person praise can create [contingent self-worth] by leading children to be proud and happy with themselves only when they succeeded, and to be globally self-denigrating with themselves when they erred. (pp. 113–115)

The techniques presented in this chapter involve a marked conceptual shift for many of us. Habit patterns of long duration keep us saying: "Good work," "I'm so happy that . . . ," or "Nice job of. . . ." I have found the results of making the change well worth the effort. When we describe young people's productive behavior to them without evaluation, we help them see that they can succeed. When we show them the positive effects of their actions, we help them conclude that they can have a positive effect on the world around them. When we avoid making them responsible for how we feel, we help them pay attention to how they feel about their own actions. When we focus our praise on positive actions, we support a sense of competence and autonomy that helps students develop real self-esteem.

Dweck (2000) writes:

Anyone who has been in the presence of children who are doing really well at something knows that there is an almost irresistible urge to tell them how good, talented, or smart they are at what they are doing. We are at a loss for other ways to show our delight and admiration. Effort praise hardly seems like an adequate substitute. But effort and strategy praise . . . can be highly appreciative of a child's accomplishments. If a child paints a lovely picture we can ask about and admire how he or she selected the colors, formed the images, and created the textures.

If a child solves a series of difficult math problems, we can ask with admiration what strategies he or she used, and we can admire the concentration that went into it. (p. 121)

In the same way, we can focus our feedback about behavior toward actions and strategies rather than toward judgments about the student as a person or toward our own feelings about the student.

Alfie Kohn (2005) writes:

[In the classroom] There's a place for unconditional love and support and attention and encouragement. That's what kids need. There's also a place for feedback: providing kids with information about their accomplishments. . . . But praise is different from either of these things. First, it's conditional: It says I'll give you attention and support only when you please me, when you meet my standards, when you jump through my hoops. Second, it's not feedback; it's judgment. And kids don't need, or thrive on, constant judgment, even if it's in the form of "Good job!" That tends to create praise junkies, who quickly grow to be dependent on someone else to evaluate what they've done. Instead, why not (a) describe what kids have done rather than judging it and (b) ask questions to help kids reflect?

Changing behavior takes practice. To help you learn the difference between the models of praise we have been discussing, I will provide some examples and scenarios. My suggested answers can be found at the end of the book. You will learn more if you think through the examples before looking at the answers.

Practice Exercises

Exercise A

1. Look at these excerpts from a frequently quoted list of ways to praise a child. Which statements focus on traits? Which focus on how the adult feels? Which focus on actions?

   A. "You're important."

   B. "You're sensational."

   C. "You are responsible."

   D. "What a good listener."

   E. "You tried hard."

   F. "I'm proud of you."

   G. "You make me happy."

   H. "You kept working until you were done."

   I. "You figured it out!"

2. Which of the following statements are trait praise? Which focus primarily on how the adult feels about the student's actions? Which are nonspecific feedback? Which are descriptive feedback?

   A. "You started work right away."

   B. "You're working hard today."

   C. "Thanks for doing a great job in class."

   D. "You have stayed out of trouble all week."

   E. "I noticed you played without fighting today. "

   F. "You are so considerate."

   G. "I saw you stay in the game without fighting when Tim yelled at you."

   H. "I am so happy that you have been kind to people this week."

   I. "You kept working until you were done."

J. "You have gone four weeks without teasing anyone. I'm proud of you."

K. "You're a good citizen."

L. "Good work!"

Before moving to another set of exercises, I will introduce one further concept. If we have time, we can go beyond telling students what we observe. We can also give them permission to feel pride, acknowledge their struggles to improve, and/or point out the natural consequences of their actions.

| Giving permission for pride. |

We can give students *permission to feel pride.* It is difficult to change behavior. It is hard to resist provocation, use self-control, persist with challenging schoolwork, and follow directions from adults. We can let young people know that they have the right to be proud of their behavior. I am not a great believer in using the phrase *"You must be proud of yourself,"* as I find that it is often ineffective to tell other people what to feel. "You have the right to be proud of yourself" is more to the point. Even better, in my view, is "That wasn't easy." This intervention will only work if we mean what we say. When we realize how hard change is, we are in a position to help young people feel proud of their own behavior.

| Helping youth take credit for positive behavior. |

We can help young people *see their actions as part of a conscious effort to improve.* When we point out patterns of improved behavior and label those as part of a plan, we help young people see their actions as intentional. We can say, "I notice that you have been staying out of fights. That tells me you are working on getting along with people" or "You are starting schoolwork right away and sticking to it until you are done. That tells me you are trying to learn."

Often young people respond to these statements with a smile. Sometimes they are surprised. Often they continue the positive behavior pattern. A change that had not been intentional becomes so.

Most effectively, we can *help young people see the natural positive consequences* of their actions, which they may or may not be aware of. I am not suggesting that we tell young people what we think will happen if they continue the positive behavior but that we tell them what we observe happening as the result of their actions. We can tell students, "Now that you are staying out of fights, you get to spend more free time with other kids" or "I notice other kids are sitting with you more." When we point out what we observe, we encourage students to notice the positive effects of their behavior. We help them make cause-and-effect connections between their actions and the effects on them and those around them. As students see that their positive actions help them reach their goals, they are more likely to continue those actions. I once heard a Southern humorist say: "Everybody's favorite radio station is WII-FM: What's in it for me?" Behavior change based on enlightened self-interest can be stable and autonomous. What all of these forms of acknowledgment have in common is that they focus on helping young people see their improved behavior as a way to meet their own needs, rather than as a way to please adults.

> Help young people see the natural positive consequences of their actions.

Exercise B

For each of the following five examples, determine which of the following three techniques the staff member is using to acknowledge positive behavior:

A. Giving the student permission for pride.
B. Seeing the student's behavior as part of a conscious effort to change.
C. Pointing out a natural consequence of the student's actions.

1. Allie teases and hits other students in the hall and at lunch. As a result, she rarely gets to eat with the other students because she earns lunch alone through the school discipline system. She goes for a week without an aggressive incident and the counselor says to her, "You have solved problems without hitting all week. You'll be eating lunch with your friends."

2. Jay often teases younger and less popular students. Afterward, he claims that he didn't do it or that the other student harassed him first. School staff want him to stop teasing and be honest about his behavior. A teacher sees him sitting with less popular students at lunch and talking with them in a polite way. The teacher says, "Jay, I noticed you talking and sitting with Annie and Dylan. That tells me you are working on being kind."

3. The principal is sitting with Ricky after Ricky hit a younger student. Ricky rarely admits to harassing behavior. When the principal asks, "What did you do?" Ricky says, "I hit Jimmy." The principal says, respectfully, "You told me the truth. I bet that wasn't easy."

4. Margaret often shoves other students if they are "in her way." She is rough in bus lines and hits or pushes others who have looked at her wrong. A playground supervisor sees Margaret in a crowd of other students who are joking together without teasing. Margaret joins in, laughs, and engages in some good-natured bantering while maintaining self-control. The supervisor waits until Margaret is separated from her peers and then says, "I saw you joke around with the other kids without hitting. That tells me that you are working on controlling yourself."

5. Jon rarely does his work in class. One day he begins his schoolwork right away and continues until he is done. He does his work carefully and competently. The teacher says, "Your work is all done. Now you won't have to take it home as homework."

Exercise C

In the next set of examples, which statement or statements use effective praise?

1. Bobby shuts down when anyone tries to correct him in any way. If peers working with him in class question anything he does, he yells at them. If a teacher corrects his work, he stops working. If asked about his aggressive behavior, he stops talking. His teacher sees him working with another student and accepting feedback about a team project. Which of the following statements should the teacher use to acknowledge Bobby's positive behavior?

   A. "I noticed that you listened when Jen asked you to redo your picture. That tells me you want to do a good job."
   B. "Great work with Jen today!"
   C. "I was so happy to see you and Jen getting along in class."
   D. "You listened in class today."

2. Jean often criticizes the work of students less able than herself. She brags about her grades and about how few mistakes she makes. An aide notices her encouraging peers. Which of the following statements should the aide use to acknowledge Jean's behavior?

   A. "Great job in class today."
   B. "You've been encouraging other students all week. That shows me you are working on being kind."
   C. "Thanks for making the class a peaceful place."
   D. "When you told Meagan that you knew she could do it, you made her smile."

3. Cody rarely makes it through the school day without hitting someone. He argues with peers and adults at every opportunity.

A staff member on morning hall duty sees him walk into school smiling. The adult asks him to take off his hat and he does. Another student asks him for help opening her locker and Cody helps her. As Cody walks off to class, the staff member wants to tell him he's starting the day well in a way that he won't argue with. Which of the following statements should the adult use?

A. "You're starting out the day right."
B "I like the way you came in today."
C. "You walked in with a smile this morning."
D. "Thanks for taking your hat off."
E. "You helped Tabitha get her locker open."
F. "I see you're happy today."

4. A group of three girls tease and exclude a peer who has a disability and often comes to school smelling of urine. They complain loudly about sitting anywhere near her, talk about her on the playground, and make fun of her to her face. They have received consequences and seem to see little wrong with their behavior. You hear that they have gone a week without teasing her and have sat with her at lunch. Which of the following statements should you use to acknowledge their behavior?

A. "You've been kind to Mary this week."
B. "I notice that you've stopped calling Mary names. That shows me you're working on staying out of trouble."
C. "I notice you've been sitting with Mary and talking with her this week. I see her smiling more."
D. "I really appreciate your leaving Mary alone."
E. "You're doing much better with Mary this week."
F. "Nice job."

5. Brett pays far more attention to other people's work than he does to his own. He criticizes peers, tells them how to do their work, and bosses others throughout the school day. You see him

working quietly in art class, absorbed in his own drawing. Which of the following statements should you use?

A. "Nice work in art today."
B. "You focused on your own work. Look at the painting you made!"
C. "You worked on your own painting. That tells me you are working on letting other people do their work in their own way."
D. "You didn't tell anyone else what to do in my class today. Thanks."

All these praise statements can be said to students quietly as we pass their desks, written on a note or a paper, or made as we pass them in the hall.

As we use methods of praise that help them build intrinsic motivation and that strengthen their ability to face challenges, we also build bonds of friendship with them. Students see that we care enough about them to take the time to point out their positive actions. In the next chapter we will discuss other strategies for building staff-student relationships.

Suggested Reading

The works of Dweck (2000) and Deci (Deci & Flaste, 1996) are highly recommended for people wanting to extend their ability to promote motivation, effort in the face of adversity, and durable change. Bluestein's (2003) article is a thought-provoking view of how we talk with young people.

CHAPTER 7

BUILDING STAFF-STUDENT CONNECTIONS

Reciprocal caring and respectful and participatory relationships are the critical determining factors in whether a student learns; whether parents become and stay involved in the school; whether a program or strategy is effective; whether an educational change is sustained; and, ultimately, whether a youth feels he or she has a place in this society. When a school redefines its culture by building a vision and commitment on the part of the whole school community that is based on these three critical factors of resilience, it has the power to serve as a "protective shield" for all students and a beacon of light for youth from troubled homes and impoverished communities.

—Bonnie Benard (1995)

Many of us can remember a teacher, a neighbor, a clergyperson, or another adult who believed in us and helped us get through a difficult time in our lives. When I ask in my workshops how many teachers remember a teacher who made a difference in their lives, half the hands in the room go up. When I ask how many of them told those teachers that they made a difference, only a few people raise their hands. We help many students every year, often without knowing the positive impact we have.

We can help students when we build connections with them and act as positive role models. The U.S. Department of Health and Human Services' Report on Violence in Schools found that adolescents who viewed their teachers as providing both academic and emotional support were less likely to experience alienation from school or emotional distress.

The report suggested ways in which to create these bonds, including

> creating one-to-one time with students; using appropriate self-disclosure; having high expectations of students that convey a belief in their capabilities; networking with parents, family members, friends, and neighbors of students; building a sense of community among students within the classroom; and utilizing rituals and traditions within the classroom. Underlying all these strategies . . . is the communication of dignity and respect through "a considerate tone of voice and receptive manner when speaking to and about students . . . taking time to listen to students and taking their concerns seriously," and conveying the message that they trust students are doing the best they can, given their developmental level and life circumstances. (Davis, 1999)

The Norwegian researchers Roland and Galloway (2002) described good classrooms as well managed and as having positive social structures. Teachers of well-managed classrooms are described by students as caring and capable. They monitor homework, behavior in class, and behavior during breaks. These teachers intervene when students behave in unacceptable ways toward each other. Classrooms with positive social structures are those where students are included and supported by peers, where students focus on schoolwork during class, and where there are clear class norms about supporting each other and doing schoolwork. Roland and Galloway found that classrooms meeting these three criteria had significantly less bullying than classrooms that did not. These differences existed even in classrooms where bullying had not been discussed.

I invite you now to assess your own school climate. Look at the following questions and decide how many of them describe your school:

- Do adults initiate positive social conversations with students? Do they greet and praise them?
- Do adults talk with students respectfully? Do they model respect and inclusion for all?
- Do adults acknowledge improved behavior? Is that acknowledgment specific?
- Do adults spend time with students in activities that they both enjoy?
- Do adults mentor at-risk students?
- Do adults give and accept feedback about each other's behavior with students?
- Do staff members maintain a positive emotional tone with students?
- Does the school protect time for adults to interact informally with students?

When we greet students, we can always find something positive to comment on. We can mention a new shirt, a haircut, seeing
them with a friend, something good they did the day before, a smile,
or their punctuality. Individual teachers can choose to greet students as they enter the classroom. School staff as a whole can agree
to greet students throughout the school. However we choose to
greet students, this intervention is effective only if we mean what
we say and are truly glad that every student is present.

All students deserve to be respected and included in class activities. When adults model respect and inclusion, students are likely
to imitate them. Since school staff are constantly dealing with a
complex network of job pressures and relationships with colleagues,
parents, and supervisors, we can lose sight of our own feelings of
frustration and anger. If we are not careful, we may take those feelings out on our students. Fred Jones (2000), in his wonderful teacher
training programs, suggests that we check our own levels of tension often by seeing if we are clenching our teeth. We may find
other ways to take our emotional temperature. However we keep
track, monitoring our own feelings is an important part of working
respectfully with youth. When we start feeling frustrated and angry,
we are at risk for dumping that anger on our students.

Positive statements about the behavior of our students should
outnumber negative statements. As I have already discussed, effective positive statements are specific. Some schools structure "caught
ya doing something good" slips or "pride slips" to help keep track
of good behavior and increase the rate of praise. Sometimes students who receive these slips are then eligible for prize drawings.
As a counselor in Vermont pointed out to me, the main benefit of
such programs is not the prizes but an increased frequency of specific praise.

Many schools have class meetings, advisor-advisee times, or
activity times. These programs offer opportunities to build relationships that can make teaching and learning more productive.

When I ask teachers about these programs, though, staff reactions are often lukewarm. I believe that the difficulty often lies in the choice of activities for these programs. As in parenting, the key to developing staff-student relationships is to spend time together in activities both adults and youth enjoy. Schools where advisee groups have the freedom to choose activities that staff and students enjoy benefit from more productive and enjoyable advisee time. If I were to design an advisor-advisee program, I would model it after activity times set up in a middle school where I worked.

> A model for advisor-advisee programs based on shared interests.

Staff members, including custodians and the superintendent, identified activities they enjoyed doing with students. Students were then able to choose from a list of those activities, without seeing the names of the adults who were leading the activities. Students and adults spent activity time together in small groups. Basing an advisor-advisee program on shared interests makes bonding between group members, and between students and staff, more likely.

The program goals of an advisor-advisee program should be clear. We should be sure that program practices continue to work toward the goals we have set. The following goals are a good place to start. First, we can strive to connect each student with at least one staff member and with a group of peers. Second, we can strive to involve all in community service projects and thus build a sense of belonging and significance. Third, we can make time each day for students and adults to talk and listen to each other.

The following story will illustrate the value of taking time to listen and talk with students. At the Bean school, Nancy Reynolds, the principal, graphed aggressive behavior over time. She found that aggression peaked during the weeks when grades closed. During those busy times, teachers have less time to hear about changes at home, the

> Effects of educators' listening to students.

new puppy, someone's sadness about an ailing grandparent, or the many other events of a child's daily life. When Nancy asked non-classroom staff to spend more time on the playground and at lunch interacting with children during those times, grading weeks no longer showed an increase in aggressive behavior.

Mentoring is another way to connect at-risk youth with adults. Formal mentoring programs link school staff or adults from the community with at-risk students. There are several ways to choose youth to be mentored. In middle school and high school these youth may be identified by asking each staff member to list those students with whom they feel a connection. The students whom no one mentions can be put on a list to be mentored. In elementary schools, teachers can nominate students. Critical to the success of mentoring programs are a commitment to consistent follow-through and ongoing training for mentors. The risk we run in mentoring programs is that mentors may not follow through on their commitments. When they fail to follow through, young people are likely to experience loss and disappointment and to blame themselves for the end of the relationship. This is especially true for youth who have had many disrupted relationships already.

| Silent mentoring. | To overcome the drawbacks of formal mentoring programs, informal or silent mentoring programs assign students to staff who volunteer to provide them with informal positive attention. |

Staff members say hello to the students they are mentoring more often than they greet other students. They go out of their way to notice when these students display good behavior. They remember students' birthdays and acknowledge their accomplishments. Silent mentoring programs are easier to set up than formal mentoring programs, require less paperwork, and are less likely to lead to feelings of loss and disappointment when mentors become busy and are temporarily unable to follow through on their mentoring commitments. Most important, students conclude that silent mentors are talking to them because they like them.

Although it can be difficult, it is also important for staff members to give and accept feedback about each other's positive and negative behavior with students. This practice helps staff remain aware of how they are interacting with students. In most schools I have visited, teachers tell me that staff members rarely give each other feedback. Constructive negative feedback is especially rare. They tell me that it is not their place to point out disrespectful behavior toward students. Without that feedback, though, we may not recognize how our behavior is hurting students. I talked with teachers in Orland, Maine, who were determined to help each other maintain positive communication with students. They decided that they wanted to know when they were "losing it" with students and talking angrily or disrespectfully with students or staff. The question was, how were they to alert each other without diminishing another teacher's authority? Since their small school has only two phone lines, the teachers decided to tell their colleagues, "You have a call on line three" to let them know that they needed to take a break, breathe, and calm themselves. Now they have a way to provide each other with needed feedback.

> Giving feedback to other staff members— a method.

There are several reasons why this kind of feedback is important. One of them can be illustrated by a seemingly unrelated story. A friend of mine was a police officer in St. Louis. He told me stories of working with partners who were abusive or disrespectful to people on the street. He told me that he had to talk with his partners about their behavior, or else *he* was likely to become the target of violence from those people. In the same way, teachers who respect students are likely to suffer under the impact of students' anger at other teachers.

The main reason I see for giving feedback to colleagues is this: What do youth learn when they see us passively allowing teachers, aides, or other staff members to be abusive or disrespectful of students? When students see us watching silently, they assume we don't care about them.

Having said this, I believe that the best way to build staff-staff communication is for us to give each other specific positive feedback. We should tell colleagues what we see them doing right, using the same model of acknowledgment I discussed previously. "I noticed that you made your expectations clear. I saw that the kids did what you asked" helps others become more effective teachers while building staff connections.

One final story illustrates the importance of positive staff-student interaction. I led a workshop for bus drivers about improving behavior. When I was preparing this workshop, I wondered what techniques could possibly work for bus drivers, who have to watch the road and so have a limited ability to focus attention on students. I asked the drivers what they had learned about improving bus behavior. Some mentioned having a simple procedure for reporting behavior infractions. Others talked about the importance of follow-through from bus supervisors and principals. One older gentleman in the back raised his hand and told us, "I say something to each student as they get on the bus. I say something about their trumpet or their new coat or their baby brother. When I remember to do this, I have good bus rides." He paused for effect. "When I forget, halfway through the ride I notice that the kids have built a campfire in the middle of the aisle and are roasting marshmallows over it."

In addition to the material in this chapter, I encourage you to read the material in chapter 9 about maintaining a positive emotional tone with aggressive students. The techniques described there apply to our connections with young people who challenge our authority in class or whom we find hard to like for other reasons. We will be more successful when we are aware of our frustration and anger, track student progress, and recognize when our expectations are unrealistic.

Suggested Reading

Aronson (2000), Brendtro, Brokenleg, and Van Bockern (1990), and Benard (1995) are useful resources for extending our work in strengthening connections between adults and youth.

CHAPTER 8

EFFECTIVE DISCIPLINE

Enforced rules can make the difference between law and order for all and the reign of terror that exists in many schools. If rules vary from one teacher or one setting to another, the students can, with some justification, challenge them. Variations provide an alibi for rule infringements. Consistent enforcement of the code of conduct requires active vigilant supervision and is one of the most effective and economical prevention strategies.

—Dorothea Ross (1996)

This chapter will introduce general strategies for effective discipline to reduce aggressive behavior. The next three chapters will discuss strategies for maintaining a positive tone with aggressive students, detailed techniques for discipline, and an example of a rubric-based discipline system.

The power of natural consequences.

Let's begin with the basics. How do young children learn to behave? Consider, for example, how young people learn to wear mittens when the weather is cold. The three-year-old may say to her father, "I don't want to wear my mittens." Her father may decide that it is not cold enough to insist. He says to his daughter, with a smile, "You know what your body needs." Fifteen minutes later, when the child realizes her hands are cold, she may want to put on her mittens. The father again says, smiling, "You know what your body needs." The child learns from natural consequences and not from a struggle between child and parent. The parent-child relationship is strengthened by this learning process because the parent can commend the child for learning. The learning is durable because anyone else who goes outside in the same temperature also gets cold. The longer the child stays outside, the colder her hands get. In learning from natural consequences, there are no other factors to interfere with durable cause-and-effect learning. Without power struggles or anguish, children learn efficiently and relatively painlessly. Children are more likely to remember the lesson.

We are not always willing to let young people experience the natural consequences of their actions. For example, our daughter Julia resisted wearing her bike helmet, but we wouldn't let her leave the house without it. One day she left our house on her bike to go swimming, towel draped over the handlebars. Between our house and the swimming hole, the towel caught in the spokes of the front wheel and stopped the bike abruptly, sending Julia head-first onto the asphalt surface of the road. The natural consequence of not wearing a helmet could have been brain damage. As it was, her helmet split in two and she walked home. How do we duplicate the benefits of natural consequences when we do not want young people to experience the natural results of their actions? We can do this by creating consequences that are similar to natural consequences in one critical way: inevitability. We might, for example, tell a child who refuses to wear a helmet that her bike will be locked up for a month if she rides without a helmet once, that her bike will be locked up for two months if she rides without a helmet twice, and that her bike will be sold if she rides without a helmet three times. We then follow through with these consequences, with all our children equally, no matter what the situation. We act without warnings, nagging, or expressing anger or disappointment. Over time, our children learn that we mean it when we say, *"If you . . . then . . . ."* Young people can learn from inevitable, escalating consequences without having to experience damaging natural consequences.

Which rules in your school duplicate the inevitability of natural consequences? Which rules are enforced automatically without anger or disappointment by all staff members? Which apply in all parts of the school, with all students? Which provide all students with the same consequences? If you find any such rules at your school, do most students follow them? In my experience, schools rarely have rules that operate like natural consequences. If they do, students follow them.

> Creating discipline systems that work like natural consequences.

Effective, positive discipline involves the following three elements: a positive emotional context; inevitability, clarity, and predictability; and a concerted effort to identify and eliminate the unintended rewards hiding in consequences.

Effective discipline is enforced within a neutral or positive emotional context. The old expression "I like you, I just don't like your behavior" is a step in the right direction. "I like you. Your behavior caused you to lose recess (or to eat lunch away from the other children)" is even more to the point. Positive discipline disconnects what students do from our regard for them. It teaches young people to understand cause and effect.

Young people may try to shift the focus from their own behavior onto an oppositional power struggle. They try to provoke an angry or irrational response from adults. They may later use this adult response to justify their own actions. We can disconnect physically or emotionally from the struggle at these times in order to maintain a positive attitude toward them.

| Maintaining a positive emotional context in discipline. | Maintaining a positive tone includes welcoming even the most misbehaving student to school each day and maintaining positive relationships with all students. If students can only get attention through misbehaving, they are likely to choose attention rather than anonymity. In a |

more chilling context, a prison inmate quoted in James Garbarino's 1999 book *Lost Boys* said, "I'd rather be wanted for murder than not wanted at all" (p. 132).

It is important for consequences to be inevitable, clear, uniform, and predictable, and thus seen as reasonable. As Rutter, Giller, and Hagell (1998) write in *Antisocial Behavior by Young People,*

> People's responses to levels of punishment are influenced by their feelings on its fairness and reasonableness. . . . If harsh punishments are seen as discriminatory and unreasonable, the main effect may be an increase of resentment and a corresponding reduced general deterrence effect. (p. 349)

Students see predictable consequences as fair. Consequences that are seen as being "given to" students by adults, instead of being earned, are likely to be seen by students and parents as arbitrary and unfair. Consequences will also be more effective if they are connected to the behavior in some way. Since most harassing behavior happens during less structured social times (lunch, recess, breaks between classes, etc.), having students sit alone and reflect about their harassing actions during these times makes sense. It also makes these times safer for the rest of the students. Additionally, effective consequences start small and escalate if students choose to repeat the behavior. Starting with small consequences allows staff to use those consequences consistently, gain parental support, and reduce incentives for students to lie about their behavior.

Dr. William Damon (1995), director of the Brown University Center for the Study of Human Development, points out that we serve young people best when we use small negative consequences so students' attention is fixed on their actions and what is wrong with those actions rather than primarily on the consequences themselves. Most of all, expectations should be consistent so that young people cannot expect to get away with aggressive behavior.

> Using small consequences.

Grading systems provide a relevant example of the benefits of clear, well-defined expectations and consequences. When I began working in Maine schools, educators were making a transition from a grading system based on impressions and estimates to one based on objective, uniform standards, called rubrics. Earlier grading systems combined teachers' impressions of students' participation and effort with grades on schoolwork to arrive at a letter grade. This subjective grade meant something different for each student and each classroom. Schools eventually recognized the difficulties with subjective grading and created grading rubrics to specify objective, measurable criteria for grades. Though this transition involved a lot of work, the benefits of the new grading paradigm were clear from the beginning. Students and parents saw grades as coming from the actions of students rather than from the impressions of teachers. The question asked of teachers, "Why did you give my child a C?" changed to "How can my child earn a better grade?" Young people and their parents are now given more data about their progress, which helps them improve.

A parallel approach can be used with discipline. In many schools individual teachers still decide what consequences will be appropriate for each student. Different students who exhibit the same

| Discipline rubrics. | behavior receive dramatically different consequences. We may decide that one student is a "good kid" and one student is a "troublemaker." |

Students who are more skilled liars may avoid consequences by convincing us that they feel remorse when they do not. When choosing consequences in this way, we invite parents and students to blame us for the consequence we are giving rather than to see consequences as the result of behavior. When consequences are predictable and uniform, we invite youth and their parents to see those consequences as the result of the students' own actions. You will find details of a rubric-based system of rules and consequences in chapters 10 and 11.

In addition, consequences often fail when they offer hidden rewards. The following story illustrates how consequences can be unintentionally rewarding. A middle school principal asked me to

| Looking for hidden rewards within consequences. | observe detention at her school because the number of young people attending detention was increasing steadily. After spending time in the school, I reported my observations. At 2:30 P.M. students are dismissed from classes and begin to board their buses. Students assigned to deten- |

tion leave class and congregate in the downstairs hall, along with other students waiting for sports practice or other after-school activities. While waiting under the supervision of a friendly 21-year-old hall monitor, students play floor hockey, fool around, yell, and run up and down the hall. Detention begins at 3 P.M. There is no standard for student behavior during detention. Some days the supervising teacher forbids all activity but homework. Some days students can listen to music and draw. On other days, students talk to their friends or to the teacher. Some days the teacher helps students with their schoolwork. Detention ends at 4 P.M. Students return to the downstairs hall to fool around under the supervision of the hall monitor. Some students sign out to walk to the general store nearby, where they can buy cigarettes illegally, meet their friends, and talk. At 5:30 P.M. the late sports bus takes most of the detention students home. These students live in a community that covers a large geographical area. Most of them would have no other way to spend this much time with their friends. Detention, therefore, was rewarding rather than punishing for the many students. When the school modified detention so that it began at 2:30 P.M., included clear expectations for the students attending, and ended at 5:25 P.M., the number of students earning detention dropped.

Hidden rewards within school consequences can be more subtle than those in this example. For example, adults supervising indoor recess or silent lunch may talk with and nurture the students who are there. On the other end of the spectrum, adults may lose their temper with students. Many young people find anger reinforcing. They may also find that telling their parents that adults yelled at them at school makes their parents more sympathetic. Parents may use angry teacher behavior to justify their child's actions and oppose the school's interventions. When consequences are not effective, we can first look for the hidden rewards that have crept into the discipline process.

To make consequences less rewarding, adults can limit their interactions with students during detention, inside recess, or silent lunchtime. They can make the interactions they have with students during these times emotionally neutral and find other times for informal positive interaction with these students. They can remain aware of their own anger and avoid expressing it toward students. Most important, they can have consequences ready for disruptive or socializing behavior during consequence time. One way to approach this last strategy is to let young people know that time spent at recess, lunch, after school, or other times "does not count" if the students fool around or talk with others. Staff members supervising consequence time should have the authority to allow students to extend their own consequences to another day if students choose to talk or fool around. I have found that when behavioral expectations for consequence time are clear and consistently followed, students get the message, and disruption during this time is rare.

Teachers often ask me, "Why not use only positive reinforcement?" It is a good question, but I reply by saying that most students are already kind to each other because they are empathic and caring. I do not believe that we should use tangible rewards for behavior that many children display for more intrinsic reasons. Yet the concept of positive discipline is important, as it is clear that angry or aggressive disciplinarians lead to bitterness or even counteraggression by youth. We have seen "zero tolerance" programs in recent years used as tools to suspend or expel difficult young people rather than to improve behavior.

Young people who are habitually aggressive may well need rewards and recognition when their behavior improves. Despite this, changing negative behaviors requires many tools. One essential element of our intervention is a set of reasonable and escalating negative consequences, in the context of positive relationships and recognition for change. Damon (1995) points out the many false dichotomies about our work with young people that we tend to hold: extrinsic versus intrinsic interventions, reasoning versus consequences, reward versus negative consequences, and compliance versus internalization. In practice, all these techniques are necessary in combination. Damon writes that "the main problem with the internalization/compliance opposition is that internalization itself generally cannot occur without an initial act of compliance" (p. 182).

The following summary of discipline research, from the Northwest Regional Educational Laboratory (2001), addresses this question and describes the techniques we will explore in the next chapters.

> [R]esearch supports the use of the following practices, many of which are applicable at either the schoolwide or classroom levels. . . . Punishment, in some forms. Researchers . . . have found punishment to be an effective method of remediating individual misbehavior and . . . improving school order if the punishment is:
>
> - Commensurate with the offense committed. Draconian punishments are ineffective.
>
> - Perceived by the student as punishment. Punishments can sometimes be too light—or even unintentionally reinforcing to students. Effective, frequently used punishments include depriving students of privileges, mobility, or the company of friends.
>
> - Delivered with support. Students often need encouragement to improve their behavior and assistance in learning how to do so.
>
> - [Used with] counseling. Counseling services for misbehaving students are based on the assumption that target students lack insight and understanding regarding their own misbehavior. Positive outcomes have been noted by researchers as a result of . . . observing and interviewing students to determine their awareness of their troublesome behavior and the meanings that it holds for them, providing information and instruction when necessary, setting needed limits, and insisting that students assume personal responsibility for their behavior and its consequences. (Cotton, 1990)

Suggested Reading for this and chapters 9, 10, and 11

Baumrind (1966), Rutter, Giller, and Hagell (1998), and Ross (1996) are good resources for examining effective discipline practices.

CHAPTER 9

> ## KEEPING DISCIPLINE IN A
> ## POSITIVE EMOTIONAL CONTEXT

Aggressive behavior is less likely to recur if it is followed by consequences that are nonviolent but immediate, certain, and proportional to the seriousness of the offense. Violence as a means of controlling aggression engenders counter-aggression, setting the stage for further coercion. Violence is reduced in the long term if the consequences are swift, assured, and restrictive of personal preferences rather than harsh or physically painful. Aggressive children and youth are typically punished capriciously and severely—the consequences of their aggression are often random, harsh, and unfair, cementing the pattern of counter-violence. The belief that harsher punishment is more effective is a deeply ingrained superstition. If teachers, parents, and others dealing with aggression learn to use effective nonviolent consequences, the level of violence in our society will decline.

—James Kauffman (1994)

It is easy to show that we like young people who come to school full of enthusiasm, compassion, and curiosity. But in every school there are a few young people whom many teachers find hard to like. When these children are absent, there are smiles in the hallways and laughter in the teachers' rooms. The challenge we face is walking up to those difficult students the next day and saying, "I'm glad you're back. I missed you yesterday."

> The least likable young people need our nuturing the most.

All students need to know that they are needed. It is the least likable young people who need our nurturing the most. When students feel that they don't belong, they have less incentive to control themselves or learn new behaviors. Rutter, Giller, and Hagell (1998) ask the important question: "What can we learn from looking at youth at-risk who do not grow up to be aggressive adults?" They point out that aggressive and oppositional youth often provoke angry and rejecting responses from adults and that those adult responses increase the risk of further aggression. On the other hand, they found that opportunities for responsibility and success in school, as well as positive relationships with adults and peers, often lead to short-term and long-term positive outcomes.

How can we help at-risk youth form and maintain positive relationships with adults? We can spend time with them in mentoring relationships or by involving them in helping us. Perhaps most important, we can make sure that the tone of our interactions with them is positive and nurturing. As I said at the beginning of this chapter, maintaining a positive tone can sometimes be difficult. The best way I know to maintain this tone involves looking carefully at the reasons that we get frustrated or angry with difficult students.

Claudia Jewett Jarratt, the author of *Helping Children Cope with Separation and Loss* (1994), offers a helpful way to look at this issue. The core of the 1980s seminar that I attended was the idea that when we, as professionals, feel ineffective in working with students, we are likely to deal with that feeling of ineffectiveness by rejecting students. Her belief was that our natural feelings of ineffectiveness are the main reason that teachers or therapists don't like young people. This transfer of feelings happens in an unconscious way, with adults often unaware of the reasons that they dislike students.

I have since observed this pattern in many professionals, including myself. When we search for the roots of our feelings of anger and frustration with a student, we often find our own sense of failure. When we see this pattern in other teachers or counselors, Jewett Jarrett suggested, we can help them recognize their students' progress and set more realistic expectations. After all, our influence over student behavior is limited by many factors we don't control. Even under the best circumstances, changing behavior is a slow process. Think of deeply entrenched behaviors you have tried to change in yourself. Maybe you have tried to change your eating patterns, the way you react to your parents, or your behavior in an intimate relationship. These kinds of changes are neither easy nor rapid. Young people have been learning their own behavior patterns for many years. If we expect rapid, sweeping change, we will inevitably be disappointed. If we pay attention only to the negative behaviors while losing sight of students' progress and strengths, we set ourselves up to dislike them.

> When we are angry at students, it may be that we feel defeated or ineffective. Are we missing small signs of progress?

Here is an example that illustrates this topic. I work with an experienced and compassionate educational technician named Sharon, who was working in a one-on-one support position with a nine-year-old boy named Cory. She came to me for help because Cory started to threaten her and increasingly refused to follow directions. She asked me to observe her interactions with Cory to see if she was contributing to his behavior. I noticed that she would abruptly walk into his body space and use an angry tone of voice to give directions. He reacted by becoming tense, holding up his fist, and beginning to argue. I told Sharon that, although I had observed her with many students, I had never seen her interact with students in this way. We acted out what I saw, and she, playing Cory's role, almost hit me when I reenacted her behavior. I asked Sharon if she could pinpoint when her behavior toward Cory had changed.

She told me that she went to a special education workshop, where she was told to document student behavior. After that, she bought a notebook and started recording everything Cory did wrong. We looked through the notebook together. The descriptions of his negative behavior began as brief statements and became more detailed and angry over time. In some of the recent entries the pencil had driven through the paper. It was clear that paying attention only to the negative side of Cory's behavior was having a significant effect on Sharon's feelings of competence. These negative feelings were influencing her behavior toward Cory and thus influencing his behavior toward her. We shredded the notebook and got a new notebook in which Sharon began to write down the many things Cory did right every day. Within two weeks I saw a marked change in her interaction with him and in his interaction with her. Instead of getting in his face and commanding him to go to math class, Sharon would say, from a comfortable distance, "In a few minutes it'll be time to go to math class. Yesterday you got a lot of problems right." Instead of arguing, Cory stopped what he was doing and went with her. As this story indicates, it is often important to ask colleagues to help us understand why we are annoyed or angry with young people, how we are expressing that anger or annoyance, and how we can shift our perspective so we see the real progress our students are making.

We also benefit from having a clear sense of best practices so that we can examine our own actions and be confident that we are doing everything we can to help.

Persistent feelings of anger toward a student are a sign that something is wrong. Anger is like the red oil light in a car. Ignoring the red light and continuing to drive will destroy the engine. Ignoring our anger at students may lead us to reject or attack them, which may provoke counteraggression. When we see ourselves becoming angry, we should stop what we are doing and find out what is wrong. There are several strategies to follow when our anger alerts us to a problem. We can keep track of what young people are doing right. This may involve tracking progress toward a goal or noting positive actions. We can ask someone else to observe our students periodically to help us recognize the incremental progress that is often invisible when we work daily with youth. We can collect data by keeping track of positive actions in a notebook.

We may easily become accustomed to each level of positive functioning and forget how far a child has come. I remember the parent whose son was referred to me because the boy would storm out of the house and break windows in his neighborhood after being asked to do chores. A few months into treatment the father came into my office angrily. "It isn't working," he said. "Last night we asked Tom to clean his room and he threatened to break windows." "Did he actually break any windows?" I asked. The father relaxed and said, "I get it." Change takes time and often happens in many small steps. We often expect quicker change than the young person is capable of and are disappointed, and therefore rejecting, when change happens more slowly.

The most powerful technique I know to recognize change is to observe behavior changes from a developmental perspective. Kindergarten teachers know that few of their students will be reading fully by the end of the year, so they use a developmental sequence to track progress. The sequence involves many small steps. First, students learn some of their letters, then all their letters, then the sounds of letters and the sounds of blends, then sight words, and so on. Each of these stages can be measured so kindergarten teachers can tell if their students are making progress. We can find similar stages in the ability of young people to use self-control and care about others. They may begin by owning up to what they have done. When students have reached this step, aggressive incidents often become less intense, of shorter duration, or less frequent. They may shift from physical aggression to verbal aggression. At the next developmental step, students may show awareness of the effects of their behavior on others. Students learn to identify the goals of their aggressive behavior, then find more positive ways to meet their goals. These steps often happen one at a time and involve significant work for the student.

Each of these transitions is a step toward moral maturity and a reason for us to celebrate. When we pay attention to the stages young people go through to reach self-control, it becomes easier for us to like them and maintain positive relationships with them.

We also need to respect the forces in the lives of young people that make it difficult for them to change. Students may be living under home conditions that we cannot imagine, and the slow and inconsistent changes we see may be acts reflecting heroic effort. For example, a young woman I once knew lived alone with her father, whose untreated mental illness created a home where everything had to be done exactly as he said and where no imagination, creativity, or individuality was allowed. This girl functioned well at school most of the time but had occasional angry episodes during which she refused to follow adult directions. She once described her life to me by saying, "It's like at home everything is in black and white. As I ride to school on the bus I start letting some colors come into my world so by the time I get to school my life is in color. Then on the way home on the bus I take the colors back out so I can live in that black-and-white world again without getting hurt." She was 12 years old and was living a juggling act that would be difficult for most adults. Many students with behavior problems have lives that are equally complex. As we respect the complexity of their lives, we can celebrate the progress they make.

Maintaining positive interactions during the discipline process can be a challenge. There are several strategies that help. One is to work within a discipline rubric or other system that clearly describes expectations and consequences for aggression. When the next step is not clear, it is easy to become frustrated and to begin using anger as a disciplinary tool. That anger may provoke counteraggression and begin a cycle that benefits neither adults nor students. Knowing that repeated aggression will lead to escalating consequences helps adults avoid a sense of frustration and helplessness. It is important for us to remember that we cannot control young people's behavior. Our job is to make positive behavior more attractive than negative behavior, build skills when skills are lacking, and find ways to protect peers from repeated aggression. We follow through with consequences, acknowledge positive behavior, show students we like them, look for signs of progress, and wait.

Our anger does not benefit students. Young people learn best when they focus on how they feel about their actions rather than on how adults feel. Here is one more example to illustrate this principle. I saw a student who had been teasing her peers approach a teacher in the lunchroom. "Are you mad at me?" she asked in an embarrassed way. "I think the principal's mad at me for teasing Janet." "I guess the real question is whether you are mad at yourself," the teacher replied. There was a long, reflective pause before the student said slowly, "I *am* mad at myself." "That's what counts," the teacher said. "That's what will help you remember not to tease again." "Oh," the student said slowly, "that makes sense."

One final case example will help to illustrate both the process and gradual nature of change in antisocial youth. In this story we can see a young man moving through developmental stages as he begins speaking honestly about his actions and developing empathy. As he moved through these stages, we saw improvements in his aggressive behavior. Ted was in the second grade when I began working at the James H. Bean School. His teachers described him as "mean" and as a young man who "has no conscience." Several

> Change takes
> time.

times each week he hit students and teased peers about their appearance. He stole valued possessions from peers. Sometimes he broke those objects, sometimes he kept them, and other times he pretended to "find them" at the end of the day. Ted showed no remorse. He claimed consistently that the teacher "didn't like him" and consistently claimed that his targets hit him first or took something of his. If he hit someone, he would say, "They shoved me into him" or "I had my hand up and he fell onto it." Ted was totally convincing. Asking Ted what he had done led to repeated denials in incident after incident. His parents seemed to believe that the school was inventing tales about their son. Any consequence Ted earned would result in hours of angry communication from home.

Shortly after we started an early version of our schoolwide discipline system for aggression, Ted and his teacher came to the principal's office to talk about an incident in which Ted kicked a student in the stomach in full view of the teacher and 10 other students. "What did you do?" I asked. "Nothing," he replied. I repeated the question, and this time Ted said, "He shoved me." "I want to hear about that later. First I want to hear about what you did," I said. Ted replied, "They pushed me into him." The discussion continued. After a few more repetitions of the question, all at the same pitch, rate, and intensity as the first, Ted's response became, "His stomach hit my foot." His next answer was, "I fell and my foot hit his stomach." Then he answered, "My foot hit his stomach." I resisted the temptation toward sarcasm and asked him again. The next time, Ted let out a long sigh. "I kicked him." Together we called Ted's mother and he told her what he had just told me.

Ted's behavior improved. Incidents of aggression continued but were somewhat less frequent and less intense. Ted was now able to describe his aggressive actions. He continued to justify his actions by referring to the behavior of others. He also began complaining of harassment from others. Teachers and administrators investigated his allegations thoroughly. Sometimes the allegations were substantiated and the other students earned consequences. More often the allegations could not be proven. Teachers and administrators continued to investigate every allegation that Ted had hurt others. Administrators told Ted's parents about the allegations they found to be false as well as those that were true. Teachers and administrators also told Ted's parents about his positive behavior, academic achievements, and situations in which Ted used self-control and honesty. Ted's parents continued to refuse to meet with the counselor or to work with the school to change Ted's behavior.

One day in the fourth grade, Ted was playing a board game with four other students in my office. The phone rang on my desk. I turned my back to the group to answer it, told the person I would call her back, and was interrupted by the sound of another boy, Derek, screaming Ted's name. I turned around and asked Ted, "What did you do?" "Nothing," he said. I turned to one of the other students in the group to ask, "What happened?" This student told me that, as Derek was taking a long time to move his game piece, Ted slammed his own hand on top of Derek's. I again asked Ted what he had done. "I shoved Derek's hand down onto his piece." "What was wrong with that?" I asked. "I'm going to get in trouble, right?" he replied. I agreed that he was, as I began to write out a behavior report form. "Was there anything else wrong with shoving Derek's hand down on the piece?" I asked. "It might have hurt him," he said. This was a big step for Ted. "Did it hurt him?" I asked. "How should *I* know?" he replied. "What do you think?" I asked. At this point Ted did the most remarkable thing. He put his own left hand over the plastic game piece as though ready to move it and slammed his other hand down on top of his left hand with considerable force. "Ow!" he yelled. After a pause, he said quietly, "It *did* hurt him." There was no sarcasm in his voice. The room was quiet, all of us appreciating Ted's moment of realization. I finished writing up the report of his aggression so he would receive his consequence and commended him on his honesty.

After this incident, we saw another decrease in the frequency and intensity of Ted's aggression. He continued to hit others from time to time, but this hitting was in the context of peer-to-peer conflict. The next year, when Ted was in fifth grade, he had three minor incidents of aggressive behavior all year. He tolerated frustration and resolved problems with words. His claims of others' aggression toward him stopped.

Changing entrenched patterns of aggressive behavior, especially without support from home, can take a long time. As we persevere and take note of small indications of progress, we can help young people to learn and use new behavior patterns.

CHAPTER 10

THE DISCIPLINE PROCESS

[R]esearchers and practitioners have identified a number of components of systematic programs to shape positive and address negative behaviors in schools. . . . These include . . . a set of well defined, equitably enacted consequences and clear, fair procedures for addressing students who break the rules. Schools need to have a behavior management system that has procedures that students understand and consequences that are clear and fair. Such systems make the process of dealing with rule-breaking more successful and easier to administer.

—Kent Peterson (1998)

There are many ways to organize discipline interventions. For reducing peer-to-peer aggression I have found it most productive to use a three-step process:

1. Report aggressive behavior. Every staff member should have a clipboard with brief report forms on it. You will find one such form in chapter 11. For peer-to-peer aggression that does not represent an ongoing risk to others, staff should send the form to the office as soon after the incident as possible. If the student's continuing aggressive behavior presents a risk to others, staff should send the student to the office.

2. Investigate, look up consequences, assist the student in calling home, and complete a letter home. For peer-to-peer aggression, this step is often the responsibility of an administrator. I recommend that a small number of people be responsible for this step, to ensure consistency of this crucial intervention.

3. Support reflection. While young people are sitting quietly for a consequence (inside recess, lunch alone, or detention), trained staff assist students in writing about what they did, reflecting on the effects of their behavior, identifying the goals of their actions, and finding other ways to meet those goals.

In this chapter, I will present strategies and techniques that I have found helpful in following steps 1 and 2. Chapter 12 will discuss step 3 in greater depth.

Step 1: Report aggressive behavior.
If staff members see aggressive behavior that breaks the school rules, they write a brief and specific description of the behavior. "Jim has been rough with other kids" or "Janine was mouthy to Richard and harassed him" do not help the administrator to enforce discipline. "I saw Jim punch Tammy in the stomach at morning recess today" or "I heard Janine call Richard an idiot" are more specific and more helpful.

If the behavior is reported to staff by a student, staff should first thank the student for telling them. I believe we should encourage youth to report aggression toward themselves and toward others. We want young people to grow into adults who will report assault, sexual harassment, and hate crimes to the police rather than ignore these behaviors or take the law into their own hands. When behavior is not seen by staff members, it is important to get a list of other students who were nearby in case it is necessary to interview them later.

Either way, the reporting staff member's next step, if this is feasible, is to ask the student who was reported to be aggressive, "What did you do?" This question, instead of "What happened?" begins the process of full accountability for behavior, as it requests a description of the student's actions. If students own up to hitting, teasing, or otherwise harassing, staff should write down what they say. If students go partway to owning up, and if the staff member has time to take this process a bit further, he or she can ask students to restate what they said, leaving out words such as "only" and "because." If staff members observe the aggressive behavior and students deny that they did anything wrong, it is important to avoid a power struggle. The young person may find that an argument with adults distracts adults from focusing on the aggressive behavior. Worse, students may be able to bait the adult into saying or doing something unprofessional and thus get their parents' support in a battle with the school. If students deny they did anything, write down their exact words and leave it at that.

Just after an aggressive act is often the wrong time to engage in moral reasoning about students' behaviors. Since the students do not yet know what their consequences are, asking questions is unlikely to lead to genuine reflection. We are more likely to hear attempts at the "right answer"—attempts to show us that students feel remorse and so do not "need" consequences.

If students present an ongoing risk of harm to others—if, for example, they are clearly still very angry and vowing revenge— they should go immediately to a safe space to cool down. If the students' actions did cause real harm but there seems no risk of the behavior continuing, we may have the students sit apart from the activity in progress for a time. Either way, we submit the report form so the next step of the process can take place.

Step 2: Investigate, look up consequences, assist the student in calling home, and complete a letter home.

If a staff member sees and clearly reports a student's aggressive actions, there is no need to investigate what happened. If behavior is reported to a staff member but not seen or heard by an adult, we need to investigate if students in question deny that report is true. It is important to have a standard form for investigation. One such standard is for the administrator to interview six bystanders separately. If all six witnesses report the same sequence of events, and if there is no sense of collusion between them, the administrator concludes that the report is valid. Having a standard method for investigation ensures fairness and allows administrators to justify their conclusions if challenged. Whether we have to investigate or not, our goals for the discipline interview are these:

- When we ask, "What did you do?" students state what they did as a simple sentence starting with "I," such as "I said Jonathan wets the bed every night."
- Students look up their consequence on the discipline rubric and tell the administrator or designee what their consequence is and what their consequence will be if they continue the behavior.
- Students call a parent and tell that parent what they did and what consequence they earned.
- The administrator or designee completes the letter home during this discussion, sending a copy to the student's teacher, two copies home (one to be returned signed), while filing a fourth copy.

If the behavior was not witnessed by a staff member, it is helpful to present incentives for honesty. When students answer that they did "nothing," the interviewer can say:

> Karen, I have something to do at my desk, and I will ask you again in a minute. If you did tease or hit and if you tell me about it yourself, I will be able to tell your parents that you told the truth. If, when I ask you again, you still say you didn't do anything, I will talk with all the other students who were nearby and do my best to find out what really happened. If I find you did tease or hit someone, I will tell your parents that you didn't tell me the truth.

The administrator should then walk across the office to do something else. Brief emotional and physical disconnection allows students a chance to save face, reduces the chance of power struggles, and encourages students to reflect. The interviewer can return after a short time and ask the student again, "What did you do?" We have found at the Bean school that most students will own up to their behavior at this point. Students are more likely to be honest about their own behavior if they believe that the school will follow through with an investigation, if they know that rules and consequences are administered fairly for all students, and if the administrator maintains a positive tone during the interview.

When students continue to say they did nothing wrong, it will not help for the administrator to judge the relative honesty of the person reporting the aggressive act and the person who is alleged to have been aggressive, based on their reputations or based on intuition. If we do that, we risk rewarding students who are more accomplished liars.

We work toward convincing aggressive students to acknowledge their behavior as a first step in the process of taking responsibility.

If students have not acknowledged what they did before the investigation, we describe the investigation process we have gone through and offer them another chance to own up before we call their parents, again offering the student a chance to help us say something positive about them as part of the phone call. Students will almost always acknowledge their actions at this point.

When students talk about others' actions that "caused them" to hit, tease, or exclude during this interview, it is most effective to tell them that we will deal with those actions after the current interview is over. I believe that we are best able to deal with aggressive behavior when we hold each student responsible for his or her own actions, rather than trying to determine who started the incident. The concept that students are responsible for their own behavior, even if they were provoked, is crucial for students' learning. We can say, "I want to hear about what *she* did later. Right now we are talking about what *you* did. Even if someone was calling you names, you had many different ways to react to that." After the investigation process is over, we remember to ask about what other students did to initiate the aggressive behavior. In my experience, most young people who blamed others for their actions decline to talk about the others' behaviors at this point. We often realize that their complaints about the other person were a distraction. If they do tell us more about the other person's actions, we start the investigative process again with the other student.

When students have told us directly what they have done, or we have determined that they have been aggressive and that they will not tell us what they have done, they are ready to look up their consequences on the school discipline rubric. I have found that having the discipline plan posted on the wall helps, as it becomes clear that the student is receiving a consequence from the school rather than from the individual administrator. The underlying message, that every student at the school who hurts others gets the same consequence, helps students understand that consequences are earned rather than given.

Next, students are ready to call a parent. Sometimes young people need to practice this talk a few times with the administrator before calling home. Our goal is to have students tell their parent(s) what they have done and what consequence they earned. Then the administrator gets on the phone and tells the parent that the student has or has not been honest. If the student was not honest at the beginning of the interview, the administrator finds something about the student's actions to commend. That way the student tells the parents all the bad news, and the administrator gets to be the one pointing out something good. Sometimes we have to interrupt the talk and remind students to read their own words off the administrator's notes. I recommend that the adult use the one phrase, "I knew you'd want to know," early in the conversation. This statement establishes a positive tie with parents, makes it clear that we are not blaming them, and lets parents know that we are not demanding that they punish their children.

In the final phase of the interview, the administrator completes a letter to parents. There is an example of a form letter in the next chapter. This letter should include details of the student's actions, the consequence earned, and consequences that will be earned if the student chooses to repeat the behavior. The letter should be signed by the administrator, the student, and the parent.

An interview following this format can be very brief and still accomplish its objectives. Done properly, this interview helps students in four important ways:

- First, since students have (we hope) chosen to acknowledge their aggressive actions, they have told two people what they did. This acknowledgment is the first step in taking full responsibility and thus in changing.
- Second, students have learned that their consequences are results of their own actions rather than statements of how the school feels about them or an arbitrary punishment.

- Third, students have learned that the administrator still likes them, even though they have done something wrong. This prevents students from being alienated from the school community.
- Finally, students have been praised for their honesty, which encourages them to be honest in the future.

The next stage of this process, which includes helping students reflect on and learn from their actions, will be discussed in depth in chapter 12. Chapter 11 presents one school's specific procedures and forms for discipline.

CHAPTER 11

A RUBRIC-BASED
DISCIPLINE SYSTEM

Our strength as a school is our ability to maintain positive relationships with all our students and not take their behavior personally.

—James H. Bean School statement
of discipline philosophy (2002)

This chapter will present the details of a rubric-based bullying prevention program that my colleagues and I have developed at the James H. Bean School over the past seven years. The Bean school was a K–6 school and is now K–5. The school has approximately 350 students. Like many rural schools in New England, our community has a wide range of income levels and relatively little racial and ethnic diversity.

The Bean school bullying prevention program works to integrate the following strategies to reduce physical and verbal aggression.

- Uniform and clear expectations for behavior that apply school-wide.
- A discipline system for aggression that outlines predictable, escalating consequences.
- Positive staff-student interaction.
- Acknowledgment of positive behavior.
- Structured opportunities for aggressive youth to reflect on and learn from their behavior.
- Support for targets and for young people who need friends.
- Classroom instruction in emotional literacy, problem solving, and conflict resolution.
- Bystander training and empowerment.

In order to follow these strategies, the Bean school has trained the entire school staff in a discipline system that helps young people solve problems without hurting each other. Consequences for hurting are predictable, fair, and immediate. We encourage staff-student involvement and positive staff-student interaction. Staff model positive interactions, include all students, and protect targets of harassment. We have developed an after-school activities program as well as a staff-student mentoring program.

We help aggressive young people to think about what they have done, what was wrong with their behavior, what they were trying to accomplish, and how else they can meet their needs. We work with young people with continuing behavior problems through school-parent teamwork, counseling, and reward for improved behavior. We support targets of bullying. We teach classroom lessons exploring compassion for others, how to express feelings in a positive way, solving problems respectfully, and supporting peers as active bystanders. We have monthly "peace day" assemblies to welcome new students to our school, talk about the values of our school, and celebrate the work students and adults do to make our school a safe and respectful place. We build peer support through encouraging students to speak up to bullies, tell adults when they witness aggressive acts, and reach out in friendship. We welcome new students by having peers introduce them to each other. Isolated students are the focus of friendship teams that help build friendships.

In her 2000 *Family Therapy Networker* article about the James H. Bean School, "Teaching Kids to Care," Dr. Mary Sykes Wylie writes: "A school like Bean may provide both a stabilizing moral and emotional foundation for children and a significant antidote to an often destructive, even poisonous mass culture" (p. 35).

The rest of this chapter will contain a collection of documents that dictate the details of the discipline approach we have developed; these include our statement of philosophy, procedures, reporting and recording forms, the discipline rubric, and the format within which students reflect on their behavior. I have also included a letter we sent home as we started the 2003–2004 school year. I invite you to use these documents as a guide as you develop a system that reflects the needs, strengths, and resources of your school. Let me stress that ours is a rural school with a small budget and no grant support for this program. Our main resource is a capable, empathic staff who are willing to try new approaches and to continue them if they work.

On the next two pages you will find samples of behavior rubrics for peer aggression. Both rubrics use the same definitions of aggressive behavior, in the following three categories. I encourage you to create your own definitions.

Teasing (name-calling, insulting, or other behavior that would hurt others' feelings or make them feel bad about themselves)
Exclusion (starting rumors, telling others not to be friends with someone, or other actions that would cause someone to be without friends)

Hitting (pushing, slapping, grabbing)

Severe hitting (punching, kicking, and similar behavior that may injure others)
Threat of serious violence
Harassment (racial, ethnic, or sexual name-calling or other severe harassment)

Because teasing and exclusion are hard to define, a written warning from the principal is a helpful first consequence. Each school should rewrite rubrics to reflect needs, community standards, staff consensus about expectations, and resources.

How quickly the consequences in a rubric escalate depends on many factors: age of students, resources available, and the extent of the behavior problems. I suggest setting consequences at a level that will remain consistent rather than using consequences that are more severe but which you will be tempted to reduce for "good" students.

A frequently asked question concerns how much time will be required for investigation and assigning consequences. Many schools using this discipline system have found that young people are likely to own up to their aggression once they know that the principal will investigate, so most interviews are brief. Most schools

have found that there is a three- to four-week period in which many
behavior reports are submitted, followed by a dramatic decline (as
much as 85 percent) in the frequency of aggression as young people learn that consequences will be assigned consistently.

A Sample Grades 1–6 Rubric for Peer-to-Peer Aggression				
Behavior	First time	Second time	Third time	
Teasing or exclusion	Written warning. Student calls parent.	One inside recess. Student calls parent.	Three inside recesses. Student calls parent.	After three incidents, develop individual plan.
Hitting	One inside recess. Student calls parent.	Three inside recesses. Student calls parent.	Five inside recesses. Student calls parent.	After three incidents, develop individual plan.
Severe hitting, threats of violence, or severe harassment	Three inside recesses. Student calls parent.	Five inside recesses. Student calls parent.	Classes only for three days. Student calls parent.	After three incidents, develop individual plan.

- Students in grades 1 and 2 receive one additional warning.
- "Inside recess" means the student stays in at one recess each
  day, completes the Think-about-It Form during that time, and
  goes outside at other recesses. "Classes only" means the student stays in at lunch and at all recesses under supervision.
- Severe behaviors may lead to more serious consequences.
  District policies may lead to more serious consequences for

severe hitting, threats, and harassment. If the student has broken the law, the school will inform the police.

A Sample Middle School and High School Rubric

Teasing or exclusion	Written warning. Student calls parent.	One quiet lunch. Student calls parent.	Three quiet lunches. Student calls parent.	After three incidents, develop individual plan.
Hitting	One quiet lunch. Student calls parent.	Three quiet lunches. Student calls parent.	One day classes only. Student calls parent.	After three incidents, develop individual plan.
Severe hitting, threats of violence, or severe harassment	Three days classes only. Student calls parent.	One week classes only. Student calls parent.	In-school suspension until individual plan is developed.	After three incidents, develop individual plan.

- "Quiet lunch" means that the student eats lunch away from peers with no interaction with other students.
- "Classes only" means the student stays alone at lunch and at all other unstructured times under supervision and participates in no sports or other extracurricular activities.
- The supervisor of quiet lunch will assist the student, as needed, to complete the Think-about-It Form.
- District policies may lead to more serious consequences for severe hitting, threats, and harassment. If the student has broken the law, the school will inform the police.

This statement of philosophy and responsibilities in the discipline process has evolved through staff discussions. It guides us in our everyday work, and we review it every fall. The key issue is that we know what to expect of ourselves and each other.

Bean School Discipline Outline

Our strength as a school is our ability to maintain positive relationships with our students and not to take their behavior personally. We maintain good behavior best when we greet students, tell them specifically what they do right, and have clear, specific expectations in our classrooms and in other situations. We maintain good relationships with parents by telling them what their children are doing right on a regular basis. In dealing with misbehavior, the most important strategy is a mental one. We remember that a student's misbehavior or refusal to do schoolwork is not about us. This focus helps us to discipline with a positive tone and without anger.

Student misbehavior falls into six categories. Each type of behavior requires a different response from school staff:

1. Low-level peer problems not on our list of rules (low-level, mutual friendship conflicts not involving name-calling, exclusion, rumors, or threats). We can respond to these behaviors with a suggestion of ways to resolve the problem (play with someone else, tell the person you want to be his or her friend, meet with the counselor together).

2. Quiet, nondisruptive refusal to do schoolwork. Notify parents after two incidents. Set up a conference between teacher, parent, and counselor and/or special educators after three incidents to develop a plan and/or screen for learning difficulties.

3. Inappropriate but not aggressive or unsafe actions (rough play or swearing not directed at another child). These behaviors are best dealt with by staff-created consequences such as removal from the activity or a call to parents.

4. Bullying (name-calling, systematic exclusion, rumors, threats, or hitting). Use immediate consequences such as "You hit, you sit" for kindergarten and first-grade students. Each staff person should have a clipboard, and outside staff should take a clipboard out to recess. Write up and submit a behavior report form if you see, hear, or have this behavior reported to you. You do not have to investigate students' reports to you, though you may ask for more information if you have time. The principal will investigate student-reported behavior. Aggressive students should be sent directly to the office only if they represent a continuing threat to others. Use your judgment in reporting rumors, exclusion, and "fighting." Please lean toward reporting if the behavior seems one-sided and likely to hurt. If there are three such incidents, schedule a conference with parents, principal, and counselor to plan a strategy.

5. Class disruption (disrespect to teacher or disrupting others' learning). Suggested interventions include a warning or asking the student to sit away from other students in the classroom. If the behavior continues, send the student to your partner's classroom for 15 minutes and have him or her stay in at the next recess detention as a consequence. Inform the counselor that the student received this consequence. Inform parents of events. If there are three such incidents, schedule a conference with the principal to plan a strategy.

6. Severe behavior (putting one's own or others' safety at risk, continued disruption of teaching; refusal to leave the room, continued or severe aggression, threat of severe aggression). Call or take the student to the office immediately.

Responsibilities of all staff schoolwide:

- Acknowledge effort, courtesy, consideration for others, and other positive behavior. Let students know what they are doing right.

- Maintain a positive tone in interactions with students and parents.

- Greet and talk with students in the halls.

- Be a silent mentor to one student (optional but recommended).

- When students report friendship troubles that are not against our rules, help them think about how to solve those problems or refer them to guidance for support.

- Keep your clipboard handy and report bullying behavior to the office on the behavior report form.

- If you are on duty, have clear expectations for student behaviors—such as listening to adults, playing safely, and eating neatly—and use your own consequences, such as having students sit away from the activity when those expectations are not met. Talk with the principal about students who break these rules habitually.

Classroom teacher responsibilities:

- Have clear classroom behavior expectations.

- Use consequences for classroom disruption and disrespect to you. Communicate with parents about this behavior. If any student has three incidents of any of these behaviors in a year, initiate a meeting with the principal or guidance counselor to set up a plan.

- Send specific positive notes home to parents about students' behavior (optional but recommended).

- If a student in your class has three confirmed incidents of aggression to peers (you will get a notice from the office), set up a meeting to develop a plan involving parents, principal, and counselor.

Principal responsibilities:

- Investigate all reports of aggression to peers.

- Determine consequences from the rubric.

- Assist students in calling home.

- Assist teachers in developing interventions for students habitually defiant or disruptive.
- With teachers, parents, and the counselors, develop and find ways to implement individual plans for students who are repeatedly aggressive to peers.
- Assist teachers in setting up and troubleshooting classroom behavior systems.
- With the counselors, clearly communicate behavior expectations and the discipline process to parents and students at the beginning of the year.

Counselor responsibilities:

- Work to resolve peer conflicts.
- Assist teachers in setting up and troubleshooting classroom behavior systems.
- Talk with students about their behavior.
- Work with at-risk students, individually and in groups. Develop plans for repeated aggression.
- Work with parents needing support.
- Develop and teach classroom guidance lessons focusing on inclusion, friendship, problem solving, goal setting, and sticking up for others.
- Develop a range of extracurricular activities to build students' bond to the school.

This form is used by all staff to report peer-to-peer aggression to the principal. Students are sent directly to the office only in situations in which there is a continuing risk of harm.

Sample Behavior Report Form

Use to report:

1. Hitting/kicking/other physical aggression
2. Teasing and other forms of verbal harassment
3. Exclusion

Student: _____ Grade: _____

Teacher: _____

Staff member reporting: _____

Location: _____ Date and time: _____

___ Witnessed by me   ___ Reported by students: Who?

_____

If you did not witness the behavior, which other students were nearby and did witness the behavior?

_____

Description of events: (Please be specific.)

_____

This is the letter we send home when a student has been aggressive.

A Note from the James H. Bean School

Dear _____,

As children develop through the elementary years, they are learning how to treat others and how to meet their needs in positive ways. I am writing to let you know that your child, _____, had a learning experience in school today. I knew you'd want to know.

THE DETAILS

1. *What was reported:*

2. *How _____ described his or her actions:*

3. *Investigation (if needed)—how I investigated, what I determined happened:*

    To help all our students treat each other safely and respectfully, we have a set of consequences for actions that could hurt someone else (see the other side of this letter). Your child's consequence is

_____.

    If _____ does this again, the next consequence will be _____.

Please sign and return this letter so I know you have seen it. Let me know if you have any questions.

Thank you.

_____   _____

Principal or designee   Date

_____   _____

Student   Parent

This is the format for the reflection process, which is done after students know their consequences. We have found that focusing on these questions as part of the investigation process is also helpful, but that the largest benefit comes from using them after the process of investigation and assigning consequences is completed. At that point there is less incentive for students to try and guess the right answer and more likelihood that they will actually reflect on their behavior. Students who are in recess detention complete this form. The supervisor of that consequence works with them, helping them to edit their answers over and over and asking them to redo what they have written until they have taken responsibility. We work with students during this time to help them acknowledge their actions, discover and feel the effect of those actions on others, and find new ways to reach the goals they were working toward through the aggressive actions.

Sample Think-about-It Form

Name: _____ Date: _____

What did you do?
Please be specific. Start with "I." Tell me later about what the other student did.

What was wrong with that behavior?
Whom did you hurt? How do you know you hurt this person?

What problem were you trying to solve?
Did you want attention? Did you want to be left alone? Were you trying to have fun? Were you already mad about something else?

Next time you have that problem, how will you solve it without hurting anyone?
Please list three ways to solve the problem.

This is the log form on which we keep track of young people assigned to inside recess. When we tell students, "This time inside doesn't count if you make noise," we are communicating something quite different from when we say, "If you make noise one more time I am keeping you in for another recess." The first statement puts responsibility on the shoulders of the student. The second makes the loss of another recess the result of an adult's choice.

Sample Inside Recess Log

Week of _____

Name	Grade	What did he or she do?	TAI form done?	Dates

We let students know that inside recess time counts only if they arrive on time, sit quietly, avoid interacting with each other, and complete the Think-about-It Form accurately. If they fool around, play, talk with each other, or refuse to complete the form correctly, they are choosing to stay in for more days, and we add those days to the log with a note. If students do not show up for inside recess, we let their teachers know. A student who is in school but who misses one day of inside recess earns one additional day the first time and two additional days of recess after that. Students not in school that day will do their inside recess time the next day they are in school.

Here is the letter we sent home to all parents as we began the 2003–2004 school year. We continue to revise and adjust this system annually to enlist parent support and to let parents know of changes in advance.

Sample Letter to Parents

Dear Parents,

Every year we review our procedures for helping kids learn positive ways to get along with and help each other. The James H. Bean School has become a national model as a kind and peaceful school. We thank you for the parent support that has made that possible.

We know that as children develop through the elementary years they are learning how to treat each other kindly and how to meet their needs in positive ways. Our guidance program and many activities within classrooms help reinforce the positive messages about how to solve problems that we know our students get at home. We also know that learners sometimes make mistakes. For the past four years we have had a set of rules and consequences to help students make good choices. Students who choose to hurt others spend some time sitting quietly and writing about what they did and what else they could have done.

We will continue to combine small consequences for unkind behavior with praise and other kinds of recognition for kind behavior. Our students have told us that they feel safer and that they are much less likely to be hit or teased than in the past. You will find a copy of the school rules about teasing, hitting, or otherwise hurting others on the back of this letter. Please call if you have any questions. The one change we plan for this year is to revise the letter that we send home if a student hurts someone. We'd appreciate your reactions to it. Thank you for your support of our efforts to make our school a safe and positive place for everyone.

School staff and faculty

Guidelines for School Discipline Systems

Since the first edition of this book was published, I have kept track of frequently asked questions about rubric-based discipline. Those questions led me to write the following troubleshooting guide for school discipline systems.

Are the rules clearly defined?

When rules are general ("We will treat each other with respect"), it is difficult to get consistent enforcement. Each adult will have a different definition of the desired behavior. When that is true, students will experience the rules as changing every time they move from one part of the building to another. Young people who experience constantly changing rules are less likely to take responsibility for their own actions. They may see the adult who punished them as the problem. When rules are behaviorally specific, staff are able to apply them consistently.

Are the school's staff committed to the importance of the rules?

Do all staff have the same understanding of what they should do when they see or hear about aggressive behavior?

These two questions point to problems in implementation. As I see it, each adult in a school divides student behavior into three categories. Staff report some behaviors to the office. Staff provide immediate warnings or consequences for other behaviors and report those behaviors to the office only if the behavior gets more severe or is habitual. Staff ignore some student behaviors. If a target of one of these behaviors asks for help, the staff member may give advice to the student about how to deal with the situation. An example may illustrate the distinction. Most school staff members would make an immediate report to the principal's office if they saw a student beating another with his or her fists. Some school staff members would deal with statements like "That test is so gay" by telling the student not to use the word *gay* as an insult, or through immediate consequences for this behavior. Most school staff members would not discipline a student who told another student in a kind way: "I don't want to be your friend anymore." They might advise the student who reported the behavior to find other friends or to wait and let things cool off for a day or two.

Without staffwide discussion of these practices, it is likely that each staff member draws these distinctions differently. These differences in response can lead to marked inconsistency in staff response to reports of peer aggression. One staff member may report name-calling to the principal, one may discourage it without reporting it, and one may counsel the recipient to ignore the name-calling. To get consensus on which course of action to take for different behaviors, staff could spend time discussing the different behaviors and deciding how to deal with them.

The playground supervisors at the James H. Bean School met to determine how we would deal with different behaviors. This statement was the result of those meetings:

Playground Rules and Discipline Procedure

Playground supervisors at our school praise, circulate, and make every effort to catch problems before they escalate. We want students to tell us when others are mean to them or when they are concerned about others. We may not always respond to reports of little things, but we avoid using the word *tattling* because that discourages kids from telling us about more serious things. We set limits and talk about consequences calmly and with positive feeling tone.

What are the basic playground rules?

- We don't allow hitting or name-calling, whether the students are friends or not.

- No one should shut other students out of a game or activity.
- Students should follow adults' directions without arguing.
- Students should play safely.
- If students bring toys from home, we expect them to share those toys, within reason.

If students do the following things, they stand against the wall or sit at a picnic table for all or part of a recess:

- Low-level hitting (pushing, bumping)—even if careless
- Low-level name-calling (not about intelligence, family, gender, or other serious issues)
- Not following directions
- Unsafe play

If students do the following things, they stand against the wall or sit at a picnic table *and* we fill out a behavior report form for the principal:

- Repeated low-level hitting or name-calling
- Repeatedly not following directions
- Serious hitting (punching, kicking, knocking down, etc.)
- Name-calling focused on intelligence, family, gender, race, or other serious issues
- Overt defiance/disrespect to adults
- Sexually oriented behaviors—kissing, pulling down clothes, etc.
- Stealing others' possessions.

If a student tells us some other students did something on this list (and we didn't see or hear it), we ask the student what they did and encourage honesty by telling them their parents will hear that they told the truth. If they say they didn't do it, we write a report including the names of witnesses. If they say yes, we write a report and commend them on the form for their honesty.

We send students to the principal immediately when they do as follows:

- Continue aggressive behavior after we ask them to stop.
- Continue defiant behavior.
- Risk harm to others or self.

We usually expect students to deal with or solve the following problems themselves:

- When someone says, "I don't want to play with you today."
- When other people won't play the game they want to play.
- When someone won't share a toy with them.

We usually suggest that they solve these problems by playing with someone or something else.

With a large staff, using discussion to reach this type of school-wide consensus can be quite time-consuming. A middle school principal developed a better way to clarify expectations and procedures.

First, the staff review and add to a list of aggressive behaviors, described in observable terms. Here is one such list:

- Punching, kicking, and pushing down
- Running into others roughly
- Slapping, grabbing, and pushing
- Shoving and shouldering
- Touching or grabbing private parts of others' bodies
- Starting or spreading rumors (true or false statements that are likely to embarrass)

- Low-level name-calling ("You're mean," "You're no good at kick ball," "Doofus")
- Name-calling related to academic ability, body shape, or appearance
- Name-calling related to family income or family characteristics
- Name-calling related to gender, sexual orientation, race, or ethnic background
- Other sexual comments
- Use of words relating to sexual orientation or race or gender as general derogatory comments not aimed at a person ("That test was so gay," " The Red Sox played like girls this season," etc.)
- Threatening comments or gestures
- Cutting in line
- Taking possessions
- Saying: "I don't want to play with you today"
- Exclusion: Telling other people not to play with someone
- Mimicking, making faces, following without making threats

None of these behavior descriptions includes the aggressor's intent. None of them depends on a statement that the target was bothered by the behavior. We are often unable to determine intent, as young people may tell us convincingly that they meant no harm. In addition, it is often difficult to determine the effect of aggressive behavior on the target. Targets of aggression often feel under social pressure to say that the behavior did not bother them.

The different aggressive behaviors are then listed on easel paper and posted on the wall during a staff meeting. Staff are given three colors of stickers—red, yellow, and green. They are asked to place one sticker next to each behavior. They are instructed to put a red sticker next to the behaviors that they think should be reported to the office each time. They are instructed to put a yellow sticker next to the behaviors that they think staff should deal with consistently. Staff reacting to "yellow" behaviors would tell students to stop, provide consequences, and report these behaviors to the office if they are habitual. They are instructed to put a green sticker next to the behaviors that they thought staff should ignore. If targets ask for help with "green" behaviors, staff would help the targets find a solution.

When I have used this technique, staff reach consensus quickly about how to deal with most of the behaviors on the list. For some of the behaviors, staff recommendations are mixed. At the next staff meeting, we can divide those behaviors into smaller categories. "Name-calling based on academic ability, body shape, or appearance" can become three separate behaviors: "Name-calling related to academic ability," "Name-calling related to body shape," and "Name-calling related to appearance." Another way to resolve differences involves having teachers rate the disputed behaviors by grade level. After two brief rating sessions in staff meetings, the staff often reach consensus about how different behaviors will be dealt with. The "red" behaviors then become the core of the school's aggressive behavior rubric.

This process will work best if we make it clear to people that the decisions being made are time-limited. We might say, "We are deciding how we will deal with peer-to-peer aggression for the rest of this school year. We will review these decisions in June and redo this exercise." We may not reach full agreement. If 80 percent of staff agree on how to deal with a behavior, we can accept that level of consensus as the standard for that year. These agreements between staff and administration should be reviewed at the end of each school year. When we clarify the answer to these three questions schoolwide we make significant progress toward consistency: What behaviors will we report? What behaviors will we deal with ourselves? What behaviors will we ignore or advise targets about?

Is the rubric for peer aggression separate from other discipline systems?

I have seen many schools try to mix consequences for aggression with those for defiance, tardiness, and refusal to do schoolwork. I am convinced that this idea is not a good one. There are two difficulties inherent in creating one uniform rubric to cover all types of negative student behavior. First, it is very difficult to sort these diverse misbehaviors into categories. Name-calling and not doing homework are two different kinds of behaviors. Parents and students are more likely to see a disciplinary system as unfair or illogical if it combines these behaviors. Second, teachers should be involved more directly with behaviors like class disruption or refusal to work. With those behaviors, it is productive to expect teachers and other school staff to take several steps before referring a student to the office. With peer-to-peer aggression, direct reporting to the office often works better. When we mix these behaviors in one rubric and in one reporting form, we risk confusing staff and students and diluting our effectiveness.

Are the forms in use effective and clear?

I recommend using three specific forms for tracking and dealing with aggressive behavior. Each of these forms is in this book.

First, schools need a reporting form. This form should be informal, brief, and easy to fill out. Since this form will often be filled out in a hurry, and since it will usually include the names of other students, this reporting form should be used internally and not sent home to parents.

Second, schools need a letter documenting the behavior and its consequences, to be sent home by the administrator. Printing this form on four-part NCR paper saves time. One copy can be filed, two copies can be sent home (with one being returned), and one copy can be sent to the teacher. This letter should document what the student did, the investigation process if one was needed, what the student said, what the consequence is, and what the consequence will be next time if the student chooses to tease or hit again. Often schools print their behavior rubric on the back of this letter so the parent can refer to that rubric.

Third, schools need a reflection form for young people to use as they reflect on what they did and who they hurt. The process for supervising reflection is described in chapter 12.

How do staff or administrators handle allegations of aggressive behavior that was not witnessed by adults?

We may be tempted to meet with the the reported aggressor and the reported target together. We may believe that if we listen to the two of them, we can decide which student is telling the truth. If we do this, we risk ignoring real aggression or punishing young people for something they did not do. One of the two students may be a more skilled liar than the other. One may be more able to appeal to adult sympathy. The risk is greatest if a young person with a history of aggressive behavior is falsely accused by a student with a spotless record and strong ties to the school staff. If we believe that allegation with no other evidence, we may punish the first student unjustly and thus lose whatever rapport we have earned with that student and his parent.

I have found that interviewing the other students who were nearby is a more reliable way to find out what really happened. It is important that we ensure the privacy and safety of the young people who tell us what happened. We should work to build a school climate where young people know they help the school community best when they tell the truth. We can help young people see that telling the truth about a friend's misbehavior helps that friend change the behavior and thus avoid more serious trouble later in life.

Often we do not need to interview the witnesses. When young people who have been aggressive know that we will make every effort to find out what really happened, and when they know that we will tell their parents if they told the truth, they often own up to their actions. This is especially likely when we maintain positive emotional tone through the investigation process and when consequences are small, predictable, and fair.

Sometimes the outcome of our investigations is a finding of "not proven." In these situations we can increase supervision of the student or situation in question. We can insist that the accused student stay away from the reported target. We can wait for future incidents when we may be better able to find out what did happen.

Are young people who break the rules held fully responsible for their actions?

Without meaning to, we may use language that minimizes young people's sense of responsibility for their actions. When we accept a student's statement that "I hit her because she stared at me," we discourage personal responsibility. When we ask young people to "tell me what *you* did," we encourage responsibility. When students excuse their actions by telling us that they were reacting to someone else's behavior, we can remind them that they had other options.

I have heard well-meaning adults say, "I understand you had a hard time keeping your hands to yourself in the hall," or "I hear you couldn't control yourself in math class." These statements give excuses for students' behavior. Instead, we can describe the behavior. We could say, "I hear you hit two students in the hall, " or "I understand you called other students 'stupid' in class."

Many young people will describe their actions as "accidents." We can help those students to see the parallel between what they are saying and the driver who chooses to drink and drive, with no intention to hurt another person. If that driver then crashes his or her car into someone else through impaired driving, that crash is no accident.

Do adults use a positive feeling tone and recognize positive behaviors within the context of aggressive incidents?

If we use our own anger as part of a discipline intervention, we risk focusing students' attention on how we feel, instead of on what they did. In addition, students often have a fight-or-flight reaction when confronted by an angry adult. This reaction reduces their ability to reflect on their behavior. We are more effective as disciplinarians when we treat the young people we deal with respectfully and thus help them focus on what they did, rather than on how we feel about them. When we tell young people and their parents about positive actions within the misbehavior, we communicate our optimism and interest in a way that makes teamwork and cooperation more likely. For example, when aggressive students tell the truth about their behavior, this action should be recognized as a sign of progress toward change.

Do adults schoolwide model positive behavior?

Young people of all ages observe adults constantly. We should examine how the school staff use their power. When staff treat other adults and students with respect, students are more likely to do the same. When staff use frequent specific praise, students are more likely to treat each other positively. As Parsons (2005) points out in *Bullied Teacher, Bullied Student: How to Recognize the Bullying Culture in Your School and What to Do About It,* these staff behaviors are more likely when staff are treated respectfully by administrators, school boards, and the community. It may also be helpful to work together to create a staff code of conduct outlining what types of feedback, disciplinary practices, and ways of talking with students are encouraged at the school. Some schools have staff agreements in which staff commit to letting each other know when they are talking disrespectfully to students.

Are consequences being used effectively? Do they start small and escalate?

Small consequences like recess detention and silent lunch are a very important part of rubric-based interventions. They should be the early steps in an escalating consequence rubric for many behaviors. It is important that they be used effectively. Factors that might make recess detention for aggression ineffective include having the detention happen in a public area, like the school office, in which students will get a lot of attention from adult passers-by or in which they can get a lot of attention through talking out, making noise, or disrupting the secretaries' work. It is also unlikely that it will work to have recess detention or silent lunch in an isolated space without direct adult supervision. Students will then be free to interact, draw, sing, and otherwise amuse themselves. An extreme (though instructive) example of the risks in such an approach can be found in the movie *The Breakfast Club.*

In addition, I have found that allowing students to complete schoolwork during recess detention for aggression reduces the effectiveness of that consequence because it diminishes both the reflection opportunities and the boredom that can deter future aggression. Having the supervising adult argue with, lecture, or nurture the students in detention is likely to reduce the effectiveness of the consequence. Many aggressive youth are starved for adult attention of all kinds. Having the adult provide that attention during the consequence time may lead to young people choosing to earn the consequence again in the future.

Some factors will increase the effectiveness of recess or lunch consequences. Having the detention happen in a relatively isolated area supervised by an adult will reduce the stimulation and attention that go along with sitting in the school office. Separating conse-quences for aggression from consequences for not doing schoolwork allows us to maintain effective behavior expectations for recess or lunch detention. Having a set of rules for the detention or silent lunch posted on the wall helps young people regulate their own actions. Here is one possible set of rules: "Inside recess time counts only if you arrive on time, sit quietly, avoid interacting with others, and com-plete the Think-about-It Form accurately. If you fool around, play, talk with each other, or refuse to complete the form correctly, you have chosen to stay in for more days." We should then follow through with these rules in a matter-of-fact way. At the end of each detention or silent lunch period, we can ask students if they have chosen to make this time count. If they have, we can acknowledge that. If they have not, we can ask them what happens next. They are likely to tell us that they have to return for another detention. Presenting rules in this way will be more likely to build responsibility than if we tell young people, "I am giving you another detention because you made noises."

If adult supervisors give young people too much attention dur-ing detention, they risk making the detention a reward. If students successfully draw supervising adults into arguments or power strug-gles, those students are unlikely to use the time to think about their aggressive behavior. For both reasons, staff supervising detention times should have their own work to do during the detention time, to help them avoid being drawn in by young people.

How do we integrate sexual, racial, or other types of legally pro-hibited harassment into a rubric?

It is important to maintain the consequences, procedures, and legal protections that apply to legally defined harassment. Rubrics should state clearly that some aggressive behaviors are subject to other school policies and to state or federal law. If we simply call legally protected harassment "bullying," we may deny targets of these behaviors some of their rights under the law.

How is the classes-only consequence used?

Out-of-school suspension (except when used to ensure the safety of the school community) may make negative behavior patterns worse. Some students enjoy the increased freedom that suspension can bring. Classes-only is a modified form of in-school suspension in which students attend class but do not participate in the more informal opportunities to interact with peers that happen during and after school. Here is a more detailed description of that consequence, designed to be sent home to parents.

Classes-Only Consequence

Many schools use suspension or in-school suspension when students choose to hurt others. To help our students learn, our school often uses classes-only instead. Classes-only status means that the student attends all classes and stays in the office or another designated location during all recesses. The student will also eat lunch in the office or in another designated location. Students on classes-only status may read or do schoolwork quietly while in the office or other designated location.

Classes-only status may be earned through our behavior rubric or may be part of a student's individual plan. Classes-only may be earned either for a fixed number of days or indefinitely, until there is change in the student's aggressive behavior.

Indefinite classes-only status is defined in this way:

- The student will begin with classes-only status for one week.
- At the end of that week, the student will earn back one of the recess blocks or lunch for the next week if he or she has not hit or otherwise hurt peers during that week. For week 2, the student will be in the office or in a designated location for all but

one of the recess and lunch blocks. The administrator will decide which recess or lunch block is earned.

- At the end of each week after that, the student may earn back one more recess or lunch block, as long as he or she does not hurt others. If the student hits others during a week, he or she will stay at the same level. Persistent or serious aggression during any week will lead to the student's returning to full classes-only status and starting again from the beginning.

CHAPTER 12

HELPING YOUNG PEOPLE TAKE RESPONSIBILITY FOR THEIR BEHAVIOR

Parents, teachers, and other caregivers can help give young people the skills to think the problem-solving way by asking questions such as: "What's the problem?" "What happened when you hit your friend?" "How did you feel when that happened?" "How do you think your friend felt when you hit him?" and '"Can you think of another way to tell your friend what you want?" This approach . . . is in contrast to the more popular disciplinary techniques of suggesting what to do (e.g., "ask for what you want") and even explaining why ("you might hurt your friend if you hit him"). Problem-solving dialoging makes the child an active participant instead of a passive recipient. . . . In all other techniques the parent [or teacher] is doing the thinking for the child.

—Myrna Shure (2000a)

141

| Internalizing behavior changes. | As we talk with young people about their behavior, we want students to stop hurting others. We also want that changed behavior to be internalized. We want young people to choose to continue these behavior changes even when we are |

not looking. One important way to help students internalize changes in their behavior involves helping them change their attitudes about aggression as a way to solve problems. Garbarino (2001) writes, "The more kids agree with statements validating aggression—such as, 'It's OK to hit people if they hurt your feelings' and 'It's OK to hit people if they hurt you—the more aggressive they are in the classroom, on the school yard, on the playground, or in the neighborhood." This chapter will be dedicated to strategies to help young people who bully dismiss beliefs that validate aggression and move toward a more empathetic view of the world.

I believe that the primary way that young people learn how to act is through imitation. When the overall level of aggressive behavior drops in a school, individual students will be more likely to solve their problems through nonviolent actions. In addition, since young people are constantly watching the adults around them, when staff demonstrate the concept that "we don't solve problems with aggression or harassment here," they are more likely to see aggression as an unacceptable way to solve problems. When students know that it is safe to stand up for themselves in nonviolent ways because adults will intervene against aggression, they can change their attitudes about how to solve problems.

We can reduce the rate of aggressive behavior through consistent discipline programs, as I have already discussed. Consistent, escalating consequences for harassment will increase young people's motivation for change, though that motivation is often based only on avoiding punishment. Unless aggressive youth develop other reasons to stop hurting others, they may shift their efforts toward more subtle forms of harassment or find other ways to avoid being caught. In order to encourage more long-term change, we can in addition help youth move through a series of cognitive and empathic steps until they reach full responsibility for their actions. As we choose effective strategies in talking with young people who have been aggressive to peers, we can help them take responsibility for their actions, rethink their assumptions, and find other ways to solve problems or meet goals in the future.

In the hundreds of interviews I have held with aggressive youth over the years, I have often observed the following progression.

1. "I didn't do anything."
2. "I did something but it wasn't my fault."
3. "I did a little something."
4. "I got punished because I called names, hit someone, or started a rumor."
5. "I hurt Jenna when I called her stupid."

These are the stages, as I have observed them:

- Denial
- Externalizing
- Minimizing
- Accepting consequences
- Accepting the negative effects of behavior on others

The first stage is usually denial. Young people who hurt others often begin our conversations by denying that they did anything. Students say, "I didn't do anything," "They thought I swore but I actually said . . . ," or "He fell all by himself." Many times this denial is convincing, and we must remember that there will be times when young people are telling the truth and others have made up stories

> Denial.

about them. Unless a staff member saw the behavior, we need to investigate by talking with peers who were nearby. At the beginning of an investigation, we must be open to all possibilities.

As we talk to everyone who was nearby during the incident of aggression, we show students that we respect them and that it is in their interest to tell us the truth. As we show that we are willing to acknowledge honesty and to tell their parents about their honesty, patterns of denial begin to change. We have found that most students choose to tell the truth when they know that the investigation will be thorough, peers are encouraged to tell the truth, consequences are known in advance and escalate slowly, and parents will be told whether their child told the truth or didn't. The shift out of denial is very difficult for some young people. It is important for staff to acknowledge this difficulty with praise.

Sometimes students do not admit to their behavior, even when that behavior was seen by a staff member or when we have investigated fully and determined that they did hurt someone else. In that case we can still administer the earned consequence and give students other opportunities to talk about their behavior after they know what their consequence will be. Often students will "plea bargain" and deny until they know a determination has been made and until they know their consequence. After that point they are more likely to own up to what they did.

Externalizing. As young people begin to admit to their behavior, they often begin to blame their actions on other people or on unavoidable situations. This externalization of their behavior can take many forms. Some forms are obvious, such as "His stomach hit my foot," while others are more subtle, such as "I hit him because he pushed me" or "Someone shoved me and I fell onto her."

Often the externalizing sentence starts with the words *because, he,* or *she.* What these statements have in common is that they reflect an underlying belief system that places the responsibility for aggressive behavior on others. Students are telling us that they had no choice but to react aggressively. They are admitting that they hit, called names, or started rumors, but only because they had to. We may foster this belief system when we ask young people *why* they hit or hurt another person. Remember that all behavior represents a choice between different ways of solving a problem or reaching a goal and that all people are responsible for the actions they choose. Remember, too, that it is easier for young people to blame their behavior on another person's actions because then they have no need to change. To help young people move away from externalization, we can ask them, "What did you do?" and remind them to "Start with 'I'." This question, and the follow-up statement, focuses young people's attention in the right direction more effectively than vague questions, such as "What happened?" When asking young people, "What did you do?" we gently but firmly insist that the answer be a simple declarative sentence like "I called Suzie trailer trash" or "I punched Tammy in the mouth."

When young people stop blaming others for their behavior, their next line of defense is often minimizing. Through this strategy, they try to convince us that what they did doesn't really matter. At this stage, they may describe a punch as a tap, a kick as a touch, or an intentional act as a mistake. The words *only, sort of, by accident,* and *might have* are often found as part of these minimizing statements. Students can minimize the reactions of their targets by saying, "I know she wasn't hurt because she didn't have to go to the doctor" or "He didn't cry." As we work with these students, we can refuse to accept minimizing statements. We can ask them to say or write the sentence again without the word *only*. If they say they might have hit someone, we ask them if they did. If they say, "I called her a name," we ask, "What name?" I remember a young man who told me, "I touched Laurie." When I asked him where he touched Laurie, he said, "On the top half of her body." I asked him to be more specific. He said, "Near the shoulders." I asked him again, and he let out a long breath and said slowly, "I grabbed her breasts." I have found that when young people say or write exactly what they did, they begin taking responsibility for their actions in a deeper way.

Acceptance of responsibility for one's own behavior comes in two forms. Young people can accept the fact that they received a consequence for their actions. More fundamentally, they can accept

Accepting responsibility.

that their behavior hurt another person. Young people often develop the first level of acceptance before the second. I do not believe that accepting the justice of a consequence is a bad thing or that it works against the development of empathy. Rather, I have seen with hundreds of young people that acceptance of consequences is a transitional step in empathic development. When young people accept that their own actions cause unhappiness *for themselves,* they are preparing themselves for the possibility that those actions also cause unhappiness *for others.* When young people have surpassed denial, externalization, and minimization, we are ready to ask, "What was wrong with what you did?" Students often restart the same cycle they went through in talking about what they did. They begin with denial: "Nothing's wrong with it," "I didn't hurt anyone." As we ask them to think about this, their next answer is often "Because there's a rule against it" or "Because I got in trouble." These answers involve externalization, showing the assumption that there is nothing wrong with what they did but that for some strange reason adults react to the behavior. We are then in a position to ask, "Why do you think we have that rule?" The most frequent answer I get to this question is "Because someone might get hurt." Finally, we are able to ask, "Did someone get hurt?" As students attempt to answer this question, we can help them use their memories of how targets reacted to the aggressive behavior to realize what effects their behavior had on those targets.

Often adults use the question "How would you feel if someone called you that name?" This question is risky. What are we to do if students say, "I wouldn't mind." This difficulty is analogous to the problem with focusing our conversations about behavior on the Golden Rule: "Do unto others as you would have others do unto you." What if aggressive youth really do like, or don't mind, if others hit, call names, or make sexual advances toward them? A teacher at a workshop once said, "I always think of sexual harassment when I hear people talking about the Golden Rule. What if we asked a sexually harassing man, 'How would you feel if female co-workers put pornography in your locker, made comments about how hot your body was, and grabbed your butt as you walked to your work station?' At least some of those men would say that they had died and gone to heaven. Even if they would like to be treated that way, they still have no right to treat anyone else that way." Sometimes young people's reactions to the same actions they dish out are helpful and sometimes they are not. We should use questions beginning with "How would you feel if . . . ?" with great caution.

> The Golden Rule.

The rest of this chapter will be dedicated to strategies to help young people move from denial to full acceptance and empathy.

Strategies

- Use language that builds accountability and avoid language that discourages it.

- Normalize the reflection process and designate a time, place, and person to help young people reflect after they know what consequence they have earned.

- Use concrete, open-ended questions rather than abstract, closed questions, and insist on real, specific, and reflective answers.

- Focus on the process of reflection as the goal rather than on "right answers."

- Use writing and editing to maintain student responsibility for reflection.

- Acknowledge the difficulty of reflecting on one's own behavior.

- Complete the work of each stage of reflection before moving on to the next stage.

- Focus on the aggressive behavior as a failed attempt to solve real problems or reach real goals, and help youth find better ways to solve those problems or meet those goals.

- Maintain a positive tone and avoid power struggles during the reflection process.

The language we use to describe students and their behavior has a profound impact on how they see their own and others' actions. Think of the ways we talk about and to young people about their behavior. Which of the following phrases promote personal accountability and clearly show young people what they have done?

1. "Tom had a hard time in art class."
2. "Manny made noise in class because the teacher criticized him."
3. "Laura couldn't sit still."
4. "Mike made noise in class."
5. "Something must be bothering Tanya."
6. "Matt must not have taken his pill today."
7. "Jeannette hit Jack."
8. "Tara had a bad day."
9. "Jimmy had to pull a card (in a classroom discipline system)."
10. "I had to tell Jimmy to pull a card (in the classroom discipline system)."
11. "Jimmy took Roy's book."
12. "You need to stop making noise."
13. "I want you to get started."
14. "Please get to work."

Look specifically at sentences 4, 7, 11, and 14, which, in my view, promote personal accountability and show students what they have done wrong. The problem with statements such as 1, 2, 3, 5, 6, and 8 is that they encourage young people to excuse their behavior by blaming it on mood, neurology, problems in their lives, or biochemistry. It may be true that something is bothering Tanya, yet there are other students in her class who are coping with equally serious problems without hurting others. Tara may be having a bad day, yet she still chooses her own actions. Language that stresses accountability and choice is more likely to help young people understand that they are responsible for their own behavior. Statements such as 9 and 10 focus young people's attention on the discipline system rather than on their own behavior. Many times I have asked students how they will make the day a good one, to hear, "I won't get my name on the board" or "I won't get a discipline referral."

As we describe students' behaviors specifically rather than talking about just the consequences of those behaviors, we help them to focus on their own actions. Phrases like 12 and 13 complicate what we are telling students. "You need to . . . ." is a puzzling statement. Often students do not need to get to work, lower their voices, or go to class. Their minds may be telling them that what they really need to do is run, yell, or hit. What I think we are trying to say by this sentence is "It is time for you to . . . ." or "If you want to earn back lunch with the other students, you will . . . ." The same holds true for the statement "That's not appropriate." Who says? Why not just say, "Please move" or "Please stop"? Asking students to do something for the adult, as when we say, "I need you to . . . ." or "I'd like it if you would . . . ." connects to Deci's research on motivation, which shows that people asked to do something to please adults have to choose compliance or defiance (Deci & Flaste, 1996). Even if they choose compliance, when students perform tasks to please adults, they often lack internal motivation to continue that positive behavior independently. Sometimes youth choose defiance, making their response to a request an opportunity to exercise their power over adults. A simple "Please get to work" or "You may get to work now or make up this work at lunchtime" is more likely to be effective than a statement that implies that we want them to do something for us.

As we normalize the reflection process, students see that everyone who is aggressive to peers is expected to think about their behavior. It then becomes easier for them to follow the process. We can use language like, "The next thing to do is . . . ." or "Now we . . . ." to emphasize that the same reflection process is expected of everyone. Most schools I have worked with consider completing the reflection process as part of the consequence so that if students choose not to complete the reflection form satisfactorily, they choose to return at recess or lunchtime to finish it. If reflection time or "think-about-it" time is expected of all aggressive students as a part of their consequences, students are more likely to work through the steps. Along with this, I have found that structuring a time, place, and person to help young people reflect dramatically reduces the rate of repeat offenses. Talking with both the principal and the reflection room teacher gives students a chance to think about their actions with two different people, thus increasing the likelihood of real learning.

| Sequencing reflection. |

When reflection time comes *after* students know what consequence they have earned, students are more likely to be honest and to use reflection time as a learning experience. When we talk with students about their actions before they know what their consequences are, they are likely to use the conversation to try to minimize their consequences. They are more likely to deny, minimize, and externalize their behavior or to try to figure out the answers we want to hear rather than to reflect genuinely on their actions. After the investigation is over and the consequence is known, young people are freer to think honestly.

Some schools I have worked with tried rescheduling reflection time before students knew their consequences. They found that rates of repeated aggressive behavior increased dramatically. When they changed the sequence back to investigation, assignment of consequences, and then reflection, they found, as I have, lower rates of repeated aggression.

As we talk with young people about their behavior, we can choose to use questions that are abstract or concrete. Abstract questions, such as "Why did you hit Sally?" or "How did Sally feel after you hit her?" invite either abstract answers

> Using concrete and open-ended questions.

or dismissive ones. Students may say, truthfully, "I don't know." Or they may choose a defiant answer: "Because she's a jerk" or "You'd have to ask her." Concrete questions, such as "What happened first?" or "What did Sally say after you hit her?" are easier to answer, encourage young people to think about what happened, and encourage students to speak honestly about the facts of the situation.

Our questions can also be open-ended or closed. Open-ended questions, such as "What did you do?" or "What was wrong with what you did?" encourage reflective thinking and give students more freedom to come up with their own answers than do closed questions, such as "Did you hit her?" "Were you kind?" or "Was that behavior necessary?" Closed questions, which can be answered with a simple yes or no, often encourage young people to search for the "right" answer, the answer they think adults want to hear. There are times when closed questions are useful in helping young people reflect. When they are saying, for example, "I might have hurt her feelings," we can help students focus and move away from minimization by asking, "Did you hurt her feelings?" Most often, though, we will find open-ended questions more useful. As we use questions that are both concrete and open-ended, we increase the probability that young people will think about their behavior and about the effects of their behavior on others.

We should also insist on receiving real, specific, and reflective answers. Sometimes the answers we get are vague, such as "I was

> Insisting on real answers.

mean to someone," or unrealistic, such as "My plan is this: When people exclude me, I will just walk away." At these times it is our job to ask for more details. We can ask, "Tell me what you did?" "What did you say to him?" "How do you know you hurt her?" or "That doesn't make sense to me—how would walking away help?"

Other times young people are clearly saying what they think we want to hear. They may reply before taking adequate time to reflect or may answer in a singsong tone, as if reciting a memorized answer to a question. It is important to direct the focus of your work with students onto the process of reflection and not on the perceived right answers, in the same way that good science teachers concentrate on having their students inquire and learn thinking skills rather than just memorize facts. We want students to "show their work" and to show us how they reached the answer they gave. When a student says, "I hurt her," quickly and with no apparent emotion, I suggest we ask, "How do you know? What did you see and hear? Tell the story from her point of view." I am indebted to Dr. Dan Olweus, who, in discussing this technique with me, made it clear that our goal at this stage is not for young people to understand *intellectually* how the target felt, but for them to understand *empathically,* or with their feelings, what the target felt. I have found that asking aggressive youth to describe the sensory details of the target's reaction and tell the story from the target's perspective is more likely to encourage them to experience what the target experienced rather than just to intellectually label an emotion. As Dr. Olweus found in his research, the most aggressive youth are quite aware cognitively of the effects of their actions on others. With these youth we risk making them better at hurting others unless they experience empathic instead of just cognitive knowledge of the target's reaction.

We can show youth that we really want to know what they think and avoid giving them cues or hints that tell them what the "right" answer is. In the process of reflection we are teaching young people to think for themselves. Many people reading this have been trained in active listening or some other form of helping where we paraphrase or restate others' statements. "I think you are saying that you know you hurt her feelings because she was crying." This technique has many positive applications. I have not, though, found it a productive method in the context of building responsibility and helping students learn from their own actions. We risk giving youth the right answer and so stopping them from reflecting about what they have done.

I have found that young people who can read and write well enough to follow the reflection process on paper benefit from writing their answers more than they do from talking the process through with an adult. In talking about these questions with a sympathetic listener, there are many subtle cues to help youth guess the right answers and thus avoid reflection. They can read our faces, listen to our tone of voice, and otherwise figure out what we want them to say. In a face-to-face reflection process there are also more opportunities for power struggles than when youth write about what they did. Using writing also leaves a record of the thinking of young people and lets several students follow the process at one time with one adult.

Our role becomes that of a writing teacher working with a writing group—we can move from student to student, affirming good choices in thinking and language, pointing out things to be changed, but ultimately leaving the responsibility for the writing up to students. Students will benefit from reflection to the extent that they do the cognitive work involved. Coming up with acceptable answers to the questions is the student's job. Our job as adults is to help them follow the format we are working with, as an English teacher would help a student follow the rules of grammar without telling the student what to write.

It is difficult for young people, as it is for all of us, to look critically at their own behavior and work to change it. We can acknowledge this difficulty as young people own up to their behavior, examine the negative impacts of their actions, and consider other options for meeting their needs. We can commend them briefly and with a relatively neutral emotional tone for their honesty, their efforts to understand the effects of their behavior on others, and their creativity in coming up with other ways to meet their needs.

Different students will spend different amounts of time in each phase of the reflection process. Regardless of the speed of young people's passage through this process, it is crucial to help them complete one question or idea at a time before moving on to others. For example, when we help young people admit what they did and move past denial, we accomplish the most when we stay with the question "What did you do?" until students have completely overcome denial, externalization, and minimization, and have fully owned up to their behavior. If young people do not own up to their behavior, there is little to be gained by searching for empathy or trying to find other ways to meet their needs. The other staff and I who supervise "think-about-it" duty at the Bean school have found that when the process falls apart we can almost always trace the problem to the beginning. Sometimes out of our own fatigue or frustration we accept an incomplete answer, such as "I think I swore" or "They said I swore," in response to "What did you do?"

One student who began the reflection process with an unchallenged "They said I swore," ended the process with this plan: "I can make things better by writing a letter saying, 'I'm sorry you thought I swore.'" This quasi-apology is unlikely to be part of any significant change in the student's behavior. I am reminded of a member of the Maine state legislature who said a series of insulting things about the women in the legislature, implying that women could not be good lawmakers. When pressed to apologize, he wrote a letter saying that he was sorry that their feelings were hurt. After public outcry, he wrote another letter, this one more to the point. The new letter said that he knew that his words had hurt members of the House and that he would not talk about women in that way again.

Myrna Shure (2000a) lists the possible needs and desires that students are seeking to meet through aggressive behavior. Among others, students are trying to gain respect, control others, and relieve their frustration. From my experience in asking hundreds of young people, "What problem were you trying to solve?" or "What

> Helping students find goals underlying aggression.

goal were you trying to reach?" I have developed a similar list. Young people who commit acts of aggression tell me that they were trying to have fun, get other students to leave them alone or look up to them, or express anger about an unrelated problem. When we see aggression as a misguided attempt to solve legitimate problems or universal desires, then we are able to work together with bullying youth to find more positive solutions. In acknowledging that we, too, have these needs, that we, too, have to find socially acceptable ways to solve problems, and that it isn't always easy, we become allies with students in an attempt to find better solutions.

Before we look at specific techniques for helping young people take responsibility for their own actions, let me restate the importance of maintaining a neutral to positive tone and avoiding power struggles during the reflection process. We should remember to give positive feedback for success at each stage. We can tell students, "Thank you for your honesty," "I see you have been thinking about what you did," or "That makes sense to me." Some young people have learned that if they start an argument, they can stop adults from enforcing consequences or focusing on misbehavior. As Claudia Jewett Jarratt taught me years ago, many adults can be drawn into a cycle that begins when they allow children to provoke them to anger. They then react angrily, doing or saying things they later regret. In trying to make amends for their expressions of anger, they offer extra nurturing or indulgence to "make up for" having lost their tempers. Children learn that if they can engage adults in arguments, then adults will let them off the hook or do more for them. In working to help young people reflect on their behavior, we see similar patterns. Rather than think about their actions and risk feeling remorse, some young people find it more interesting to explore adults' reactions to their behavior. Young people experiment with refusing to talk, arguing, telling adults the rules are stupid, or telling adults that the child they teased deserved it.

Adults' angry reactions to these experiments may be more attractive to students than thinking about their own behavior. After adults express anger in a harsh or critical way, they may feel bad and try to make it up to students through extra attention. When adults are harsh and critical, young people may also be able to use that staff behavior to forge an alliance with their parents against us. Even if young people are not looking to manipulate the situation in these ways, our anger and criticism do nothing to help them think about how *they* feel about their actions. When we see power struggles or sense ourselves becoming angry while helping young people reflect, we can follow several strategies to avoid expressing our anger. First, through whatever strategy works for us, we can maintain calm nonverbal and verbal behavior. One way to do this is by reminding ourselves that we cannot control the behavior of students.

We should also remember to expect denial and to celebrate the small incremental gains young people make as they move from denial to externalizing, from externalizing to minimizing, and from minimizing to acceptance. As in teaching any subject, our job is to accept the young people's current level of skill and knowledge and help them move to a higher level.

We can restate the question and then physically move away from students who are trying to start a power struggle. Sometimes when we go to another part of the room, students will begin thinking and writing again. If they do not, we can let students know that they are choosing to come back on their own time, at a future recess or lunchtime, to complete the process. As young people see that we are not going to fight with them and that it is in their best interest to continue the reflection process, they often return to the task at hand. If not, we need to be prepared to try again tomorrow.

Which questions will make it most likely that young people will reflect on their behavior, develop empathy, and find better ways to meet their needs? For the past 35 years I have been wondering about this. I have found the following four questions, used in sequence, to be the most productive.

These questions can serve many purposes. They can be used as a writing exercise during an inside recess or silent lunch consequence. We can use one or more of them informally in talking about incidents with young people, or all of them as the foundations of a therapy hour. Students who find writing difficult may dictate their answers to an adult.

1. What did you do?
2. What was wrong with that?
3. What problem were you trying to solve? What goal were you trying to reach?
4. Next time you have that problem or goal, how will you solve it or reach it without hurting someone else?

I will now discuss strategies for working with each of these questions one at a time. When we ask students, "What did you do?" we can encourage them to overcome denial by saying, "Tell me about what they did later—start with 'I' now." Remember to ask at the end of the meeting what "they" did, and be prepared for the very real possibility that the answer will be "nothing." "They started it" is often a smoke screen aimed at blocking reflection.

We can help students overcome externalization and minimization by encouraging them to tell us specific details about the incident. We can ask, "Where on his body did you hit him?" "Show me with this chair how hard you hit her," or "What names did you call him?" We can ask students to write their answer again without the words "only," "just," or "because." We can insist that students edit and reedit until their answer contains no minimizing or externalizing language. Our goal for this first question is a simple sentence, such as "I punched Justin in the ribs," "I told six people not to be friends with Janet," or "I called Jimmy a retard."

When we ask students, "What was wrong with that?" students often say, "Nothing" or "I don't know." As we ask them to think about the question some more, the most common reply is that their behavior was wrong because they got in trouble or because "You have a rule against that." We can reply to this statement with the question, "Why do we have that rule?" When students reply that "I might have hurt her" or "There's a rule because someone could get hurt," we are ready to ask, "Did your teasing hurt her?" "What did he do after you called him a loser?" or "What did you see or hear after you hit him?" The goal of this second question is an answer that acknowledges that another student was hurt by the aggressive behavior. A good form of that answer is "I hurt Susan when I hit her." Better still is "I hurt Susan when I hit her. I know I hurt her because I saw her crying."

Often students will not be able to answer the third questions: "What problem were you trying to solve? What goal were you trying to meet?" in their open-ended forms. When students have difficulties with this question, asking about goals instead of problems may help. In addition, the following question is often helpful: "When people hit or call names, they are usually trying to get someone to leave them alone, impress their friends, have fun, deal with anger about something else, or be listened to. Do any of those sound like the problem you were trying to solve?" The goal of this stage of the reflection process is for students to choose a goal that the adult can honor. We may have to help students restate their goal so that we can agree that the goal is a worthy one. If students say, "I wanted revenge" or "I wanted to hurt her," we might offer them a choice of several more acceptable goals that might underlie their statements. We can say, "I want to understand. Do you mean that you wanted to be listened to, that you wanted the other person to stop bugging you, or that you wanted your friends to look up to you?" Avoid restating the goal yourself. Instead, offer several options and help young people figure out for themselves what they wanted to happen.

Asking, "What problem were you trying to solve?" should not be an invitation for aggressive students to blame the targets of their aggression for their actions. No matter what the target may have done, we can best help aggressive young people by holding them fully accountable for their own choices or actions. This question also does not imply that bullying is caused by a conflict between peers or that we can stop bullying by having the bully and the target "talk things out" with each other. Using mediation-based approaches may, in fact, make the bullying more intense by allowing bullies to blame the target for their actions or even demand concessions from the target. Rather, this question focuses on the problems we all face in life and the goals we all have:

- Wanting to have fun
- Wanting to get our way
- Wanting to be heard
- Wanting to be left alone
- Wanting others to admire us or see us as a leader
- Needing to find a way to deal with strong feelings

There are several follow-up questions we can ask students in order to clarify their response to the last question, "Next time you have that problem, how will you solve it without hurting anyone?" We can ask young people, "Will you ever have this problem as an adult?" and follow that question with "When you are an adult, what will happen if you solve the problem the same way you did this time?" We can encourage students to brainstorm three or more ways they could solve the problem and choose one that is best for them. Then we can ask them to identify a backup choice in case the first doesn't work. The goal of this fourth reflection question is a clear answer, such as "Next time when I want someone to leave me alone I will tell them politely. If that doesn't work, I will walk away." A satisfactory answer to this question is highly dependent on the previous questions. Without a sense of what problem they are trying to solve, young people cannot construct a real answer to this last question and will, in my experience, fall back on a stock answer, like "I'll just walk away." Accepting an answer like this one without a sense that it comes from reflection about better ways to solve a real problem does not help change young people's behavior. It is unlikely that the "plan" will be put into action, as it is a statement of the "right thing to do" rather than being a way to solve an important problem or reach a significant goal.

In addition to the reflection process, some aggressive students will need more intensive counseling for issues relating to family conflict, anger management, loss and grief, or poor social skills. A few will angrily, or even calmly, refuse persistently to participate in the process. Those students may have to learn from consequences alone. A substantial number of students, though, find the reflection process I have outlined here to be enough to help them change their behavior.

Building empathy is a crucial goal for all human beings. For some students, developing a genuine understanding of others' feelings is a long and difficult process. While that empathic sense is developing, these aggressive youth may change their behavior to avoid consequences from adults and because they realize that they are losing friends. It is important, though, that we keep working to build empathy.

Schools I have worked with have found that structuring opportunities for reflection makes the difference in lowering recidivism. Consistently, students who have thought about their behavior in the ways I have described are less likely to repeat aggressive behaviors and more likely to solve problems in other ways. When we help young people identify their own needs and find better ways to meet those needs, they are more likely to change than when we just tell them to stop doing something.

Dr. Nick Piazza says, in *The Rules for Counseling:*

> Progress is when a client stops doing something
> that is self-defeating. Change is when a client starts
> doing something that is more effective. . . . Client
> progress is generally for the benefit of someone
> else; client change is for the benefit of the client.
> Client progress can be an illusion. Changes in the
> way people act are what really count. (n.d.)

Practice Exercises

The following are practice exercises to help you build skills in promoting reflection. My suggested answers to the questions can be found at the end of the book.

1. Which of the following responses should we accept as answers to the question "What did you do?"

    A. "Nothing."

    B. "I only touched him with my foot."

    C. "They were calling me names so I hit them."

    D. "I pushed him on accident."

    E. "I called her a name."

    F. "You always pick on me!"

    G. "I said, 'Sarah can't wait to get home and have sex with Andy.'"

2. You are supervising detention, and students are writing about their behavior. In response to the question "What did you do?" a student who closed a peer into a locker writes, "I didn't do anything!" Which of these adult responses could work?

    A. "Please try again."

    B. "I am so sick of your denying everything!"

    C. "I think you did. Please write about why you're in detention."

    D. "Are you saying you're not ready to do this today? You can do it in detention tomorrow instead."

    E. *(Looking in the detention log)* "It says here that there's a reason you are in detention. Please try again."

3. You are supervising inside recess and students are writing about their behavior. In response to the question "What did you do?" a student who said publicly that a peer wets the bed writes, "I

made fun of him because he always takes my stuff." Which of these responses could work to move this student toward a more complete answer?

A. "Does that give you the right to make fun of him?"

B. "Two wrongs don't make a right."

C. "I want to hear about what he's been doing to you after we talk about what you did."

D. "Please write that again without what he did to you. We'll get to what he did later."

4. A student pushes another student off a piece of gym equipment, causing her to fall and get hurt. It was clearly intentional. In response to the question "What did you do?" the aggressive student writes, "I pushed her by accident." Which of the following responses could work to move this student toward a complete answer?

A. "Don't you know she's in pain?"

B. "Take some responsibility!"

C. "Stop lying to me!"

D. "You have this almost right. Please write it again, leaving out the last two words."

E. "Just write what you did."

5. Which of the following statements should we accept as complete responses to the second question: "What was wrong with that?"

A. "Nothing."

B. "I might have hurt her."

C. "I got in trouble."

D. "It isn't nice."

E. "You shouldn't do it."

F. "I embarrassed George."

G. "I made Helen feel unsafe."

H. "I scared Scott."

I. "I probably hurt Gerry."

J. "I hurt Jim. I heard him yell, 'Ow!'"

K. "It made Laura cry."

L. "I made Laura cry."

Items 6–9 present student responses to the second reflection question: "What was wrong with that?" Choose from the adult responses to each student statement to determine how best to help young people complete this question satisfactorily.

6. Student response: "Nothing."

   A. "Think about what you saw or heard after you hit Sam."

   B. "Please try again."

   C. "How would you feel if someone hit you?"

   D. "Are you saying you're not ready to do this today? You can do it in detention tomorrow instead."

7. Student response: "I might have hurt her" or "I probably hurt Gerry."

   A. "Would you stop wasting my time?"

   B. "Did you?"

   C. "What did you see her do or hear her say after you hit her?"

   D. "OK, let's go on to the next question."

8. Student response: "I got in trouble."

   A. "I am so sick of your getting in trouble!"

   B. "Thanks. Let's go on to the next question."

   C. "That's right. Why do we have rules against teasing?"

9. Student response: "It isn't nice" or "You shouldn't do it."

A. "What do you mean?"

B. "Who did you hurt?"

C. "Thanks. Let's go on."

10. A student leads a group of others in taunting a younger student (Katie) about her clumsiness. When asked what problem he was trying to solve, he says, "She's stupid." Which of the following adult responses should you use?

A. "What problem were you trying to solve?"

B. "Let's see. . . . You could have wanted the other kids to look up to you, you could have wanted Katie to leave you alone, or you could have wanted to have fun. Do any of those reasons sound like what you wanted to happen?"

C. "How can you say that? Don't you know she's doing the best she can?"

D. "You always blame other people!"

11. A student takes a treasured possession from a peer, hides it, and then "finds" it the next day. When asked what problem she was trying to solve, she writes, "No problem."

A. "Take some responsibility!"

B. "OK, move on to the next question."

C. "Here are some possible problems: You could have wanted her to like you, you could have wanted to be important, or you could have been angry at someone or something else. Do any of these sound right to you?"

D. "Try again."

12. Which of the following answers should we accept as accurate responses to the question "Next time you have that problem, how will you solve it without hurting anyone?"

A. "I'll walk away."

B. "I'll be good."

C. "I'll behave."

D. "I won't hit."

E. "I'll use words."

F. "I'll tell an adult."

G. "I won't call names."

H. "I'll control myself."

I. "I'll count to 10."

J. "I'll say something kind to her."

K. "I'll ask her to play."

Guidelines for Using the Reflection Process

Since the first edition of this book was published, I have kept track of frequently asked questions about the reflection process. Those questions led me to write the following set of guidelines for using the reflection process effectively.

The reflection process is designed to be used *only* for peer-to-peer aggression, not for class disruption, refusal to do schoolwork, or disrespect to staff. These other types of behavior should be addressed through consequences and other interventions; this particular intervention is unlikely to work with them.

Supervising the think-about-it process requires a set of skills that grow with practice. The process will be more effective if a relatively small number of adults supervise it consistently and develop their skills in this intervention, rather than having this duty rotate between many adults.

Young people do the think-about-it writing during recess detention, quiet lunch, after-school detention, or other supervised consequence time after they know what their consequence is. Using this intervention after young people have learned what their consequence is makes it more likely that their writing will be the product of genuine reflection rather than being an attempt to talk their way out of a consequence.

Students write their answers to the questions. They may write at a table or on clipboards while they face away from each other. If they have trouble writing, they can dictate to an adult. In that case, adults should resist the temptation to help by suggesting words or by paraphrasing.

The supervising adult is in the room and moves from student to student as young people tell him or her that they are done with one of the questions. Supervising adults have two primary roles. First, they ensure that young people do not make the consequence time into a reward through fooling around or interacting with each other. Second, they make sure that young people complete each stage of the think-about-it process fully before moving on to the next. If young people choose not to complete the Think-about-It Form, the supervising adult informs the student and the administrator that the student has chosen to return for another detention. We should remember that completing the Think-about-It Form is the student's responsibility rather than the adult's. The student should do 70 percent of the work; the questions and protocol 20 percent; the adult 10 percent of the work.

The supervising adult should have other things to do when students do not need help: e-mail to answer, a book to read, a report to write. Having something else to do helps the adult avoid giving the students too much nurturing attention, making the consequence time rewarding. It also helps the adult avoid the temptation to nag the students or argue with them. When students try to start an argument about completing the form, supervising adults should walk away and return to their other tasks to avoid being drawn in. We can remind students that the consequence time does not count if they choose not to complete the form fully. Students can then choose to make the time count or to refuse to complete the reflection process and have their consequence extended for additional days.

When there are problems with the think-about-it process, I have most often found that they can be traced to the first question. If a student answers the first question ("What did you do?") incompletely, the rest of the process is compromised. As I discussed earlier, I have found that students will often begin by denying that they did anything and then blame others for the behavior, writing that they hit someone because that person called them a name. Students are then likely to minimize the behavior, writing that they *only* called a name or that they pushed *a little*. If the process is unsupervised or done at home, if the supervising adult is untrained or overwhelmed, or if the student is persistent in maintaining these avenues of avoiding responsibility, adults may allow the student to move on to the subsequent questions without moving to a statement of full responsibility for his or her own actions. *I have found that refusing to accept partial statements of responsibility is the most important factor determining the effectiveness of the think-about-it process.*

Examples of a statement that meets the criteria for moving to the second question are these: "I called Jennifer a &^$%," "I grabbed Jeremy and pushed him to the ground," "I started a rumor that Mark wets the bed," and "I punched Tajandra in the face." When students do not write this type of responsibility statement, they are likely to give brief and insincere responses to subsequent questions in the process. In this case, students will be unlikely to learn anything from the process.

The art of supervising this process involves telling young people calmly that they have not yet fully answered the question they are working on. We should explain briefly what they should do to complete the question. We should then walk away and leave them to write some more and return when they tell us they are ready for us to edit with them again. I have seen English teachers use the same process in teaching writing: moving back and forth between students at work, giving brief feedback, and moving on to the next student or waiting until another student was ready.

Another problem sometimes experienced with the think-about-it process involves young people refusing to complete the questions. The best way to minimize this problem is to have the reflection process take place during recess, lunch, or detention so there is a built-in incentive to finish it and thus have the consequence end. If students are given the reflection form during time when they are supposed to be in class, they may delay completing the form to miss more class time. Having the reflection process presented as a matter-of-fact expectation for students "to help you not do it again" is more likely to work than asking students to "do this for me." "Now it's time to. . . ." may work better than "Now I want you to. . . ." In addition, it is important to recognize that some persistently aggressive youth may have great difficulty taking full responsibility for their actions. For these students we may choose to use only the first question or to make other temporary modifications in the process.

When students insist that they did *not* do anything wrong, it is sometimes necessary to arrange another meeting with the administrator to review what has happened.

If students' behavior disrupts the consequence time or provides entertainment for the other students there, it is sometimes necessary to remove them from detention and have them move to a more powerful consequence, such as classes-only or in-school suspension.

I discussed useful questions to facilitate reflection earlier in this chapter. Here is a list of those questions to be used as a reference during the process. Remember to avoid being drawn into discussion, argument, or doing the work for the student.

For the question "What did you do?"

"Start with 'I.'"

"What words did you use?"

"Where on his body did you hit him?"

"Tell me about what they did later—start with 'I' now."

"Please write this again, leaving out 'only' (or 'just')."

For the question "What was wrong with that?"

When students write, "The school has a rule about that," or "Because I got in trouble," we can say, "Yes, we do have a rule against it. . . . Why do we have that rule?"

When students write, "It might have hurt her," we can say, "Did it hurt her?"

When students write, "I hurt him," and we don't think they mean it, we can say,

"How can you tell?" or

"What did he do after you called him a *&^?" or

"What did you see?" or

"What did you hear?"

For the question "What problem were you trying to solve?"

For elementary school children, consider replacing this question with "What did you think would happen next when you did that?" if students don't seem to understand the word *problem*.

We can say, "When people hit or call names, they are usually trying to get someone to leave them alone, trying to impress their friends, trying to be heard, or trying to have fun. They might also be angry about something else. Do any of those sound like the problem you were trying to solve?" If the word *problem* doesn't apply in the situation, ask the students what goal they were trying to reach or what they wanted to happen after they called names or hit.

If students choose a goal that you cannot honor or agree with, like getting revenge or hurting someone, ask them which of the above goals they were trying to reach by hurting someone.

It can be helpful to ask young people if they think they will ever have the same problem or goal again in life. If they think they will have that problem again, ask what will happen if they keep trying to solve that problem by hurting others.

For the question "Next time you have that problem, how will you solve it?"

Ask them if they will ever have that problem again.

Ask them to brainstorm different ways they might solve the problem in the future.

Ask if each of those solutions will work, and also ask them to choose one to use next time they have that problem.

In evaluating the students' solutions to the problem, ask yourself if the solutions address the problem being solved. "Just walk away" might work as a way to deal with being angry. It won't help if someone took your ball. The solutions should be actions. "Don't do it again" gives students no guidance about what to do instead, and thus should not be accepted.

Suggested Resources

Shure's works (Shure, 2000a & b, 2001a–d) are the best resources I know for people wanting to help students learn how to think.

A Framework for Understanding Poverty, by Ruby Payne (2001), describes similar interventions and a similar reflection process, with the goal of helping young people overcome the culture of poverty.

A video demonstration of this reflection process in action is available from http://www.stopbullyingnow.com/video.htm.

CHAPTER 13

WORKING WITH PARENTS

Let your child know you're approaching the school. He or she may worry that this will make things worse—but remember that bullying thrives on secrecy. . . .

Be cooperative—say "what can we do about this situation?" rather than be accusing or angry.

Ask the school what policies they have to deal with bullying.

Ask the school how they usually cope with bullying.

Ask what you can do to help.

Before you leave, be clear about what the school will do and when they will contact you.

—New South Wales Health Department (2001)

Parents and teachers working together can accomplish more than educators can alone. Yet it is easy for schools and parents to become adversaries. As school staff, we may believe that parents are responsible for their child's behavior because of their parenting style or their denial of the problem. It is sometimes difficult for parents to work with schools. Many parents do not trust school staff. They may have had negative experiences in school themselves or struggles with other authority figures in their lives. Parents may be unsatisfied with the school's attempts to protect their children. They may believe that we do not like their children or that we fail to see their child's point of view. Parents may wish that school staff would protect or help their children more. It is easy to initiate a cycle of reciprocal blaming.

Yet it is crucial to involve parents in the intervention process as much as we can. Change is certainly possible without parental involvement, but schools and students benefit when parents are involved as equal members of the team. This chapter presents strategies to involve parents in their children's therapy and education. Many additional strategies can be found in Dr. Ron Taffel's (2001a) excellent book, *Getting Through to Difficult Kids and Parents.*

The primary techniques I have found to help build and maintain positive relationships with parents include the following:

- Welcome students and their families to school.
- Treat all students and families fairly.
- Maintain a positive tone and acknowledge the feelings and efforts of parents.
- Tell parents what their children are doing right.
- Meet regularly with parents of struggling youth.
- Find positive and important roles for parents to play as team members and give them credit for change.

- Listen to the ideas and concerns of parents and act on as many of those concerns as possible.
- At times of crisis, ask, "What would you like us to do?" instead of reacting defensively.
- Earn trust by following through on commitments.

First, welcome students and their families to school. Walk around your school imagining you are the parent of a new student. Or, better yet, have a friend who does not know your school imagine she is the parent of a new student. Evaluate in what ways visitors and students feel welcome and in what ways they feel that no one needs or wants them there. Do parents and students experience smiles and eye contact when they walk the hallways? Are parents informed about classroom activities and special events? Are they welcome to visit and help out in their children's classrooms? What do the physical layout and decorations of the building tell new parents? What about the body language of staff? These elements, and many more, determine the climate of a school as either welcoming or excluding families. Many small details, such as the presence or absence of signs showing how to find the office or classrooms or the communication style of the school secretary, will show families whether or not they are valued and included in their children's education. I recommend an annual survey and staff review of what does and does not make your school welcoming for parents.

Treat all students and families equally, using predictable and uniform expectations and consequences. The most common barrier to working with families of aggressive youth is the perception of those families that the school discriminates against their children. Those perceptions might be unjustified, but they might also be based on the parents' accurate observation that their children have received more severe consequences than other children for the same actions. Parents may claim that school staff turn a blind eye to harassment directed at their children and only notice how their children behave under provocation. It is important to remember that parents want to

> Predictable and
> uniform
> expectations
> and
> consequences
> help us earn
> parents' trust.

believe their children and want to see their children as good people. Those natural desires make it difficult to hear that their children have hurt others. We can help parents see their children's behavior accurately through several strategies. I believe that the best strategy is to use a behavior system that is transparent and predictable—in which all parties know the definition of and consequences for aggressive acts. In addition to uniformly and predictably structuring expectations and consequences, we should also apply this uniformity to the ways in which we investigate allegations of aggression. We work best with parents when we can tell them the exact steps we follow to confirm and consequate an aggressive act. Over time most parents will see that their children are being treated the same as other children. To gain and keep this trust, we must be careful always to follow our disciplinary procedures and not assume, in a conflict in which both children give different stories, that the child with the worst behavior record is lying. We earn trust when parents see that we avoid making assumptions about their children, we seek out the truth, and we apply negative consequences to aggressive behavior directed at their children.

> Maintain a
> positive tone.

As with students, it is important to maintain a positive tone with parents and acknowledge their feelings and efforts. It is easy to become frustrated with parents of persistently aggressive youth. If these parents would only set better limits at home! If they would just make the simple changes that we know they need to make, things would be so much better! The reality, though, is that most parents are doing the best they can. A participant at one of my workshops said recently, "We have to get over the idea that parents have better behaved children at home who they are choosing not to send us." Most parents are doing a better job than their own parents did with them. Some are forced to work long hours just to put food on the table. Others are stuck, along with their children, in negative cycles of behavior. No matter the reasons behind their behavior, our anger and frustration will only make matters worse. Our job is to show parents what they are doing right, make small suggestions and help parents implement them if they want to, and show respect and affirmation for their ideas and opinions. As we avoid judging parents and show that we respect them as people, they are more likely to work with us instead of against us.

In order to create positive relationships, we tell parents what they and their children are doing right. This acknowledgment is most effective when it is specific and frequent. Anyone who works in a school has had the experience of calling a parent and hearing a panicked reply when we tell the parent we are calling from the school. As the school counselor, I often have to say, "Jimmy's not in trouble right now," at the beginning of my phone call to a parent. If parents hear from school staff only when their children are misbehaving, they may begin believing that staff don't like or value their children. The same can happen when we tell them specifically about their child's bad behavior and describe the good behavior only in general, vague terms. Sending brief, specific positive notes home on a regular basis, especially for children we know are likely to misbehave, builds a strong foundation for positive collaboration with parents.

> Tell parents what they and their children are doing right.

For struggling youth, it is important to meet regularly with parents to assess progress and establish long-term and short-term goals. When we meet only because there are problems or when parents are angry, we reduce our opportunity to build working relationships. When we meet infrequently or only in crisis, parents often accumulate resentment over time and come to these meetings angry or confused. When, instead, we meet monthly for 20 minutes, we have the opportunity to build a team. Parents and educators have a chance to address small problems before they grow and review current interventions as well as plan new ones.

Find positive roles for parents, and give them the credit when things work.

Parents play important roles in helping their children change and need to have their positive work acknowledged. This acknowledgment can come in the form of helping parents find positive and important roles as team members. It is also helpful to give them credit for contributions toward their children's improvement. When parents' roles are limited to listening at meetings and signing forms, they cannot see themselves as valued team members. Parents can play many positive roles in an intervention. Parents can reward their children with extra attention at home for receiving positive notes about their behavior. Parents can urge their children to behave better and let school staff know what their children are thinking and feeling. When we pay attention to the positive results of this parent involvement and point out those results to them, parents see themselves as important players in their children's education. A quote from Harry Truman is especially applicable. He once said, "It's amazing what you can accomplish when you don't care who gets the credit." Attributing the success of students to specific actions by their parents is a valuable way to maintain positive parent involvement.

To show that we value the involvement, thoughts, and concerns of parents, we need to listen to their concerns and act on as many of them as we can. I always begin monthly review meetings by asking what concerns or questions parents have. Sometimes there are big problems; sometimes there are only questions of detail. Either way, we are often able to make small adjustments that work better for families and students.

No matter how well we build relationships with parents, there will be times when those relationships break down. At these times, it rarely helps to attempt to justify the school's actions. It is even less likely that meeting anger with anger will work. Fisher, Patton, and Ury's (1983) book, *Getting to Yes: Negotiating Agreement*

Without Giving In, is an invaluable guide to working together in difficult situations. The authors suggest a guideline for conflict resolution that is useful here—only one person gets to be angry at a time. At a moment of crisis, it is the parents' turn to be angry. Listening helps, as does a genuine apology when we have done something wrong. What helps even more is an attempt to refocus the discussion on what specific steps we can take to resolve and prevent further conflict. We can calmly ask the question "What would you like us to do?" to refocus toward working together. Sometimes parents will tell us what they want in vague terms: "I want you to respect my child," "I want you to stop intimidating my child," and "I want you to protect my child." In these cases, we will need to work together to define the specific actions parents are asking us to take and which of those actions are possible for us. Often what parents are asking us to do will help. Some of what parents want us to do will not be possible. Sometimes the actions they want us to take may be, in our opinion, against the best interests of their children. As we keep exploring parents' view of what they want us to do and what we can and believe we should do, we can almost always find ways to work together. As we commit to understanding what parents want and need instead of acting defensively, we are on the road to improving relationships.

> "What would you like us to do?" is a question to use in conflict situations.

Finally, to build trust, it is important for us to follow through on our commitments. The fundamental way to earn trust is to be trustworthy—that is, to do what we say we will do or let people know why we have been unable to do so. Taking this obligation seriously means thinking about the commitments we make before we make them, writing down what we say we will do, and following through.

I will end with a specific example of how parents can have both negative and positive effects on their children's behavior, as well as how it is beneficial to attribute improvement to the efforts of parents. Howie was the bully of the fifth grade at his school. As a result of his aggressive actions, children often came in from the playground in tears with scrapes, bruises, and bloody noses. Consequences had little effect. His father, a large, muscular, illiterate man with a long history of distrust of the school and arrests for assault, encouraged Howie's aggressive behavior. "If other kids mess with you or your younger brother, you let them have it," he said on more than one occasion. The principal and I reassured Howie's father that we would not let other kids pick on his younger son or on Howie. We told him that we knew that Howie looked up to his father and would listen to him more than he listened to us.

We told him that we couldn't let Howie beat up other kids and that there had to be consequences for hitting. Howie's father agreed to tell Howie to stop hitting other kids, but only on the condition that we agreed to protect Howie's younger brother. Staff made sure that Howie's brother was protected. Several days after this conversation, we realized that Howie had not hit another child in days. We called his father and told him that he had made the difference and that we had known that he was the one whom Howie would listen to. Howie's hitting, and his father's distrust of the school, changed dramatically from that point onward.

In Appendix B, you will find a handout for parents that summarizes the basics of bullying prevention and outlines what parents can do to raise responsible, caring children. The U.S. Department of Health and Human Services (2003) publishes a brochure you can distribute that clearly presents the essentials of the Olweus approach.

Suggested Reading

Both of Taffel's (1999, 2001a–b) books are indispensable resources for people who work with parents, as is Garbarino's (2001). Fisher, Patton, and Ury (1983) will guide you through resolving the conflicts that are an inevitable part of teamwork.

CHAPTER 14

SUPPORTING TARGETS OF BULLYING

When dealing with a bullying problem, it doesn't help to instruct the victim to solve the problem herself. Children who are persistently victimized have most likely exhausted their strategies for responding to bullying. Each time they have been bullied, they have likely tried something to stop it. By the time they approach an adult, they have likely reached the end of their tolerance because no strategy they have tried has been successful in stopping the bullying. Furthermore, peers consider it "acceptable" to bully someone with low social status. Therefore, it is essential that an adult assist the victim and intervene to shift the power imbalance between the victim and bully.

—Wendy Craig and Debra Pepler (2000a)

Remember Peter from chapter 4? His bullying problem was made worse by well-meaning adults. Here I will continue his story. Peter's parents asked me to meet with Peter to talk about how he was being treated and how he felt about himself. I was not sure what to say or ask, as I was sure that Peter had already tried every action I could suggest. Finally, I settled on asking him why he thought the bullying was happening: "Because I'm short and I talk funny?" he asked. I disagreed, asking him to think some more. "Because they think I'm gay," he said. Again I disagreed and there was a long silence. "Because they're *jerks!*" he said, sitting up taller in his seat. I agreed. Even if he was short and talked funny, or even if was gay or was perceived as gay, the fact that his peers harassed and embarrassed him was evidence that they were selfish jerks. It was not evidence that there was anything wrong with Peter himself. I told Peter that I did not know what would happen but that it was important that he not blame himself for the teasing.

Some months later I ran into Peter's mother. I asked her about Peter and she told me the teasing had stopped. I asked how that had happened. She told me that after my meeting with Peter, she and Peter's dad had gone to the school to insist on more supervision and more significant consequences for harassment. They told the school that they would call the police and press charges if the school did not stop the bullying. The school responded to their clear, forceful request, and the harassment stopped almost immediately.

Could Peter's knowledge that his bullies were jerks be enough to see him through his time in school even if adults had not protected him from continuing harassment?

Probably not, but the knowledge that the problem lay with the bullies was clearly significant for both him and his parents. This knowledge empowered the whole family to act more effectively to stop the bullying.

The story of Peter shows one way that we can support targets. We can make it clear to them that the bullying is not their fault. By helping young people understand what has happened to them, we can encourage them to stop blaming themselves.

Here is another example of this type of intervention. A second grader named Steve was teased at school. A week later, a junior high student who rode Steve's bus smeared a ripe banana all over Steve's face. Although both of these students received consequences and neither one continued the harassment, Steve's parents were concerned that Steve seemed to be taking the harassment personally. When I talked to Steve about the banana incident, I asked him, "Did the kid with the banana take it out of his bag or was it already in his hand?" "He got on the bus with the banana in his hand," Steve said. "What does that mean to you?" I asked. "That someone was going to get the banana in his face," he replied. I asked Steve to tell me where he was sitting when the banana incident took place. He told me he was sitting in the front row. "Who was sitting near you in the front row?" I asked. "A bunch of bigger kids," he said. At this, Steve nodded and said, "I get it. Thanks, Mr. Davis," and went off smiling. Steve stopped blaming himself because he was able to see this boy's behavior for what it was—an act of opportunity.

There are four additional strategies that I have found helpful in supporting targets.

- Stop the bullying from happening again.
- Think carefully before giving advice.
- Brainstorm solutions with targets.
- Recruit peers to befriend isolated targets.

One helpful way to think about these four strategies is to review what we do when we help young people who are coping with loss and grief. It is helpful to treat bullying as a loss experience and support targets of bullying in the same way we would support young people experiencing the loss of a family member, a friend, or a pet. Most of us do know effective strategies to support young people through loss, and bullying involves many losses, including the loss of safety, self-esteem, belonging, and control over one's own life.

When young people grieve, we encourage them to show and talk about their emotions rather than minimizing them, while accepting that young people may not yet be ready to show or feel emotion. Just as we would not tell children grieving over a parental divorce to "forget about it," we shouldn't tell targets of bullying, "Don't let it bother you." As we would with children coping with loss, we can nurture, spend time with, play with, and comfort young people who are bullied. As much as possible we can protect young people from other losses and traumas. For example, when young people are coping with parental divorce, we help them by preventing other losses. We help them keep in touch with their friends, maintain familiar routines, and otherwise keep the rest of their lives the same. Similarly, the primary way that we can support targets is to stop the bullying from happening again. When the bullying stops, targets can get on with their lives and recapture a sense of safety and belonging.

As Craig and Pepler point out in the quote at the beginning of this chapter, much advice that adults give to targets is useless. Often targets have already tried and failed to stop the bullying by using the strategies we are suggesting. When we suggest actions that have already proved ineffective, students may assume that either they are no good at standing up for themselves or that we are not too bright. In the worst case, they will take our advice and keep reacting to the bullying in ways that make the situation worse. This said, there is one kind of advice that helps young people. We should advise young people that silence will not work to stop the harassment and they should keep telling adults until things change.

If we want to focus with targets on what they can do to stop the bullying, we will be most effective by using a problem-solving approach. We can ask targets what strategies they have already tried and what has and hasn't worked. Then we can encourage them to discard solutions that have not worked and brainstorm other solutions. They can try these new ideas and learn from the results. This type of intervention is based on the interpersonal cognitive problem-solving skills work of Shure and Spivack (1982) and Shure (2000a–b, 2001a–d), and on the bullying prevention work of Dr. Richard Hazler (1996), of Penn State University. This strategy allows us to affirm the many efforts students have already made to stop the bullying. It also lets us give them permission to stop trying behaviors that have not helped. Brainstorming helps students come up with and try out their own solutions. We should tell targets that the bullying may continue no matter what they do and encourage them to continue telling adults if what they try doesn't work.

Helping isolated youth join an extracurricular activity or club, in which they will meet classmates who share common interests, is a powerful way to promote friendships. It can be equally helpful, if not more helpful, for targets of bullying or young people who are isolated for any reason to participate in activities with students who do not know them. In these situations, young people have the opportunity to try out new ways of connecting with peers and are able to change their view of themselves. New positive relationships can help young people build self-confidence. Theater is an activity of special value in this regard, as actors learn to reinvent themselves within each new part.

My son Ben told me about a parallel experience of his that illustrates both these points. An actor all through high school, he went away to a summer science program as a relatively introverted teenager. He later told me that he had decided to make friends by connecting actively with other students in the program. He said that, during the three-hour car ride from home to Boston, he had prepared to reinvent himself as though he were preparing to go on stage in a new role. That summer's successful experience of friendships carried over into his day-to-day life when he returned home and into his transition to active involvement and leadership with classmates all through college.

Additionally, we can recruit peers to befriend isolated students. One of our fourth-grade students invented a particularly effective way to help youth make friends: the friendship team. I will describe the use of friendship teams in chapter 16.

Provocative and reactive targets.

At this point, I will address the needs of two specific groups of targets—provocative targets and reactive targets. Provocative targets seem driven to provoke bullying by irritating their peers and seeking negative attention. Some of these students have learned to get negative attention from peers, and consequently sympathy from adults, by provoking harassment. They may not know how to get attention in positive ways or may be unable to get positive peer attention because of peer rejection. We serve provocative targets best by enforcing consequences for bullies and also for provocative targets if they break rules. Consequences for the bullies lessen the chance that provocative targets will receive the negative attention their behavior seeks out. No matter how obnoxious targets are, we should continue to hold bullies fully accountable. Additionally, no matter how peers react to them, we should continue to hold provocative targets fully accountable for their provocative behavior. Justifying either person's actions by referring to the other person's behavior will interfere with learning for both students involved.

We can also help provocative targets by teaching them new ways to get positive attention and by making sure that those ways work more reliably than the provocative methods. We will often need to prepare some generous peers to reach out to them. In doing so, we should choose students who are resilient and confident, as it is quite possible that the provocative target will seek negative behavior from these potential friends. In working with provocative targets, we should be careful to limit both sympathy and anger. Sympathy reinforces provocative behavior, whereas anger strengthens the belief that negative attention is the only kind of attention they deserve or receive. We need to be vigilant in preventing our own frustration and impatience with these children from leading us to believe that they deserve what they get.

Reactive targets are easy targets for bullies because they react so strongly to even minor incidents. Their tears, tantrums, and other overreactions reinforce bullying behavior by giving bullies a sense of power. Often these youth generalize that "I get teased every day" or "Everyone picks on me." Sometimes they have been overindulged and overprotected at home or receive a lot of sympathy whenever they express sadness. Sometimes they have been bullied so much that any new event triggers a strong reaction, just as people with posttraumatic stress disorder may react strongly to a small reminder of their trauma.

We help reactive targets when we examine our practices and cease to reinforce their behavior. Are we overly sympathetic? Do we nurture overreactive targets when they react strongly to minor hurts? We can also help reactive targets by using techniques that help with anxiety disorders. First, we help them identify small actions or stimuli that bother them and choose which of these small behaviors they want to learn to tolerate. We help them practice other responses to the small problems and learn to calm themselves using relaxation, breathing, or imagery. Second, we help them focus on the present rather than the past or the future. Instead of becoming overwhelmed by harassment and focusing on what "always" happens, we help them focus on what is happening here and now and on what they can do about that present behavior.

As in our work with provocative targets, we help reactive targets when we avoid blaming the target; maintain the use of consequences, reflection, and full accountability in working with bullies; and help reactive targets build positive friendships. We can limit sympathy and advise parents to do the same. We can also help these young people master anxiety by making sure they have one staff member they can go to for support and protection when they have a problem. We should overcome our natural response of irritation to the near-constant complaining of some of these youth. Even a reactive target deserves to be protected from harassment and needs to be heard. Finally, we help reactive targets when we encourage them to write down in a journal positive actions from others.

We support targets when we protect them from further bullying and help them to avoid internalizing the harassment. We aid them in deeply effective ways when we help them make friends and become full members of the school community.

Suggested Reading

Sanford (1992) presents the life experiences of adults who are thriving despite childhood trauma and discusses in very helpful terms how humans overcome obstacles.

CHAPTER 15

BULLYING BETWEEN FRIENDS

One of the biggest hurdles I see is that adults often don't believe kids when they tell them they have been victims of relational aggression. . . . Girls who have been victimized by relational bullying will say "This hurts," and the adults in their lives will dismiss their concerns, sort of a "Girls will be girls" version of the old saying, "Boys will be boys." In the end, girls who are bullied end up not having allies. . . . The best thing I hear about are the administrators who make it clear to teachers and to kids and parents that, just like physical bullying, relational aggression is also against school policy, and students who victimize others in this manner will be reprimanded. . . . [T]he most important step by far is to make the victims of bullying realize that adults will step forward and provide support. This is a serious problem, and we've ignored it for far too long.

—Nicki Crick (2002)

According to recent literature, bullying among girls is more likely to be a subtle part of an ongoing relationship than bullying among boys. Bullying among girls often involves social exclusion and the spreading of rumors. Simmons (2002), in *Odd Girl Out: The Hidden Culture of Aggression in Girls,* states that bullying among girls is more likely to involve constantly shifting targets. In these types of relational aggression, young people take different roles over time, alternating between aggressor, bystander, and victim. Simmons says that girls are likely to describe bullies as their friends, and Mullin-Rindler (2003), writing about relational aggression with girls and boys, says:

| Relational |
| aggression. |

> Like other forms of bullying, relational aggression typically occurs in public and often involves groups of students who gang up on the hapless victim(s) with friends against peers—further adding to the power imbalance and sense of shame and humiliation the victim feels. In addition, relational aggression may be particularly insidious because victims often allow themselves to be subjected to these acts in silence—often out of a combined desire to fit in and fear of further ostracism. (p. 7)

Mynard, Joseph, and Alexander (2000) found that the impact of relational aggression, which they called social manipulation, was more profound than that of teasing or hitting.

I have become convinced that staying in relationships that involve bullying of this type trains youth, especially girls, to accept abusive dating relationships and to call that abuse a normal part of friendship. In both cases, the aggressor oscillates between harassment and apology, between hurting and nurturing, and between enmity and an imitation of friendship.

Yoon and Kerber (2003) surveyed teachers, asking them how they would react to different types of bullying. They found that teachers described social exclusion as a less serious problem than direct physical or verbal bullying. They found teachers less sympathetic to the victims of exclusion, more likely to ignore the behavior, and less likely to intervene. The belief that we should not interfere with young people's friendships is understandable. After all, police and courts stayed out of abusive marital relationships until the late 20th century. Laws removing spousal immunity in rape are fairly recent. We realize now that being identified as a friend or as a spouse no longer brings with it the freedom to hurt or abuse.

I am writing this brief chapter to suggest some strategies I have found helpful in dealing with relational aggression, whether it happens between girls, between girls and boys, or between boys. I have found the following techniques helpful in preventing relational bullying:

- Extend the consequence system to include the more subtle behaviors involved in relational aggression.
- Help young people disconnect from abusive friendships and form more nurturing friendships with nonbullying peers.
- Encourage bystanders to refuse to be used by aggressors as assistant bullies.
- Build alternatives to one popular clique.
- Encourage alternatives to an exclusive focus on popularity and belonging.
- Encourage journaling during adolescence.

Our discipline systems can include sanctions against spreading rumors, exclusion, and similar actions. Mullin-Rindler (2003) suggests that rules about bullying should include "exclusion, ignoring, disrespecting, or making comments about someone's reputation or character" (p. 14). The consequences should apply even if young people report a day later that they are "friends again." A temporary end to the hostilities often does not signify that the problem has been resolved.

| Help students disconnect from abusive friendships. |

We can help youth see that someone who hurts them is not their friend and support them in building nonabusive friendships. I believe that this is the most important intervention of all when dealing with relationship-based bullying.

We can start building awareness of these issues in third grade, when exclusive friendships start to form, and should continue addressing them throughout the school years. In addition to helping young people differentiate between abusive and non-abusive friendships, we can help them think about which students are consistently kind to them and to see *those* young people as their friends. The most important way we can do this is to provide the friendship of a caring adult, which is an especially important part of healing. When students have support from an adult and experience a more positive model of friendship, they are more able to risk breaking free from abusive friendships and forming healthier ones.

| Discourage young people from assisting in bullying. |

In our classroom discussions we can examine the common role of assistant bully. This bystander often carries messages and tells the target hurtful things others are saying. In my experience, these youth often say they are just helping targets know what is being said about them. I sense that many of these assistant bullies enjoy the power involved in being the one who carries the secret, delivers the message, and sees the emotional reaction. They may enjoy that sense of power without taking any responsibility for the target's pain. As they realize that their actions are hurting others, many of these students will resign from the role of assistant bully. I have found it helpful to point out that if someone gossips about someone else *to* them, that person will soon be spreading rumors *about* them.

Anything we do to help youth create alternatives to one "popular" clique will help. When one group of popular students stands at the top of a single social ladder, and when many others strive to be admitted to that group, the popular youth can be tempted to use their power over others in hurtful ways. We should encourage those around the edges to form groups of their own and declare independence from the popular clique. Power corrupts, after all, and the power given to the popular youth often corrupts them. In addition to direct conversations with students about these issues, we can use literature-based discussion to explore friendship options. A useful book in exploring this issue with middle school girls is Amy Goldman Koss's 2002 novel, *The Girls,* which presents conflict and harassment within a group of teenage girls from the point of view of all the girls involved. For elementary school students, Trudy Ludwig's 2003 book, *My Secret Bully,* presents the issues in an engaging, positive way.

As we help young people to take pride in their skills and knowledge, set and work toward goals, and take learning seriously, we help them insulate themselves against an exclusive focus on popularity.

Finally, we can encourage young people to use journaling to get them through the storms of adolescence. James Pennebaker (1997), in *Opening Up: The Healing Power of Expressing Emotions,* shows us the healing power of writing about traumatic events. His research found that regularly writing about stressful events and the feelings associated with them led to improved emotional and physical health. Journaling has the advantage of allowing us to be completely honest about what we think and feel. Writing allows us to put difficult feelings away where we can always find them but where we are not bothered by them every day.

I have found the interventions mentioned in this chapter helpful as youth navigate the issue of relational bullying, most notably
by helping them disconnect from abusive friendships and build
new, healthier relationships.

Suggested Reading

Mullin-Rindler (2003) and Crick (2002) present what we know
about relational aggression at present and make many useful recommendations. Ludwig's (2003) book helps us discuss this issue
with students. Perlstein (2003) helps us see the complexity of middle school social networks—and of middle schoolers themselves.

CHAPTER 16

ACTIVATING PEER BYSTANDERS

While attention is most often directed at the experiences and traits of aggressors and victims, the majority of students (75–80%) are bystanders. These students play a key role in all types of bullying situations. Bystanders tend to feel anxious and afraid, and report that bullying interferes with their own learning. . . . 90% of students reported [that] observing bullying was unpleasant, [yet] as many as 65% of bystanders don't actively get involved. . . . Students reported that they failed to act because they felt the incident was none of their business or were uncertain about what to do. Although students may argue that not getting involved is safer . . . their inaction results in bystanders experiencing feelings of anxiety and powerlessness similar to that of victims. . . . As a result of their passive or complicit participation in bullying, bystanders may have a tendency to justify, rationalize or minimize their role. Studies also show that over time, bystanders' sense of empathy for the victim of bullying is diminished, which tends to lead them to side with the bully.

—Nancy Mullin-Rindler (2003)

A wide range of studies have found that 60 to 80 percent of all students are neither bullies nor targets. It is these students who can make a difference in a school's climate. When bystanders tell adults about bullying incidents instead of maintaining a code of silence, school staff are enabled to reduce bullying. When bystanders include and befriend excluded youth, they empower those students and help them heal. Rigby (2000) found that students who were victimized at school and who felt they could get help from friends or family were less likely than more isolated victimized children to have inferior health. Mullin-Rindler, in the opening quote, focuses on the negative effects on bystanders of watching bullying in silence. Young people all over the United States have told me how proud they feel when they act against bullying.

I have now talked with more than 40,000 students around the United States about bystander behavior. I began by training them to carry out the three bystander actions we often see in the literature: (a) I encouraged them to tell the bully to stop, (b) I told them it was important to tell an adult, and (c) we talked about the importance of reaching out in friendship.

I heard feedback from students, telling me that the first of these suggestions was a problem. When we practiced telling the bully to stop, using interactive theater, students acting as bystanders would often "bully the bully" and start a fight. Even when I coached the young volunteer actors to tell the bully to stop, using peaceful methods, many of them seemed irresistibly pulled toward an aggressive intervention. Sometimes, if the actor playing the bully was intimidating enough, I found that student actors playing the bystanders would stand frozen when they were supposed to tell the bully to stop. Some students wrote me that they would not tell bullies to stop in real life because doing that was too risky. For some years I sought ways to help bystanders overcome these difficulties. I taught them nonviolent ways to ask the bully to stop. We discussed intervening as part of a group and from a distance. Still, many bystanders seemed pulled toward aggressive confrontation during the interactive theater exercises. Many sensibly backed away from telling bullies to stop in real life. Two issues make telling the bully to stop a problematic intervention.

First, young people who watch television have seen so much aggressive confrontation that they have trouble understanding any other form of confrontation. Second, even if they learn and use less aggressive techniques for telling the bully to stop, bystanders are legitimately afraid of standing up to bullies directly. They may fear losing the friendship of popular peers. They may fear being targeted themselves. Vaillancourt, Hymel, and McDougall (2003) write:

> Supporting a victim carries considerable risk for loss of social status if the bully is both popular and powerful within the group. For most students, it may be more socially advantageous to support the more powerful and high-status bully. If so, school-based anti-bullying programs, especially those that encourage peer bystanders to intervene, will be difficult to implement. Such programs can be effective only if the peer group does not empower the bully by revering and supporting him or her. The fact that over half of the bullies in the present sample were viewed as high status (popular) and powerful makes peer support to such aggressors difficult to eliminate. (p. 18)

I realized that there was a parallel to adult life that could guide my work. What would I do if I looked in through a store window and saw a robbery in progress? I would definitely not go into the store and tell the robber to stop. This analogy has helped me to understand the advice we can give to bystanders. I have begun asking students what caring adults would do if they saw a robbery in progress.

Students tell me that I could call 911 and give the police information about the robbery. They tell me that the police would accept an anonymous report if I chose not to give my name. Students are clear that the dispatcher would not tell me I was tattling. If I gave my name or testified in court, I would be protected from retaliation.

I could help in other ways as well. As I discuss this scenario with young people, they tell me that I could keep pedestrians from going into the store during the robbery. I could help the business owners clean up the broken glass later. I could shop at that store more often. I could support the business owners in some other way. I could advocate for more police presence and organize a neighborhood watch.

I think this analogy can guide us in helping young people to support targets of bullying. We can discourage young people from telling bullies to stop, except in situations that are safe for them. We can empower bystanders to create and use a wide range of safer and more effective alternatives, including telling adults, helping targets get away from bullying, and befriending targets in other ways. Before we encourage bystanders to tell adults, adults should be prepared to respond to reports and protect these youth from retaliation.

I asked a group of high school students what they want adults to do about bullying. They said:

> "Let us report bullying with protection—privately and confidentially."

> "Welcome our reports and act on them."

> "Form strong positive relationships with us so we feel free to report bullying to you."

"Don't be afraid to take action to stop bullying."

"Listen—keep your eyes and ears open."

How do we make it safe to tell adults about observed incidents of bullying? To explore this issue, I would like to return for a minute to adult parallels. When adult witnesses report crimes, for

> Making it safe to tell.

example, they are performing a task similar to the one we ask of peer bystanders in schools. Why do witnesses report crimes? They report because they believe that police will take them seriously and will listen to them, that effective action will be taken against the perpetrator of the crime, and that they will be protected from retaliation. When witnesses do not report crimes, it is often because one or more of these factors are missing. Targets of bullying want and need the same kinds of support as adult witnesses, especially when it comes to protection from retaliation. We can institute anonymous methods of gaining information, like drop boxes or telephone message lines. These methods are helpful in the early stages of a bullying prevention intervention, when young people do not yet believe that they will be protected from retaliation.

In addition to battling the previously discussed fears that students share with adults, young people also struggle with the connotations

> "Tattling."

of "tattling." The concept of tattling as a negative behavior makes bullies more powerful by discouraging youth from telling adults about incidents of bullying. How do we undo this empowerment of bullies? I have seen teachers explain the difference between telling and tattling by saying that telling is what we do when someone is being hurt, while tattling is something we do when no one is being hurt. Teachers I met in San Diego have an even better way of conceptualizing the telling versus tattling issue. They say to their students, "We want you to ask for help, both for yourself and for other people." This way, if a student reports that someone is hitting another student, it is clearly a request for help. If a student tells the teacher that someone has three pencils—something that the student thinks is unfair—it is clearly not a request for help. I would rather have us discard the word *tattling,* as this word is used by bullies to torment their peers with "You little tattletale!" When we use the word *tattling,* we risk not hearing from youth who really do need our help. Thorne (1993) writes:

> There is a . . . stereotypical association of younger kids and of girls of all ages with complaining to adults about the behavior of other kids. The word "tattling" is often used for this behavior, which conveys the telling of tales, secrets, and thus the betrayal of one's kind. The negative connotation builds in a judgment I want to query. Sometimes the less powerful, or those not trained to be physically aggressive, have little recourse except to complain to adults. (p. 77)

Rock, Hammond, and Rasmussen (2002) quote a student who describes why he did not tell teachers about bullying incidents: "Telling a teacher is like tattling and we have a rule in our class about that. And you have to have witnesses and everything. It's easier to just settle it yourself." On the surface, "just settle it yourself" sounds like a good idea. Don't we want youth to solve their own problems? As we look at parallels to other forms of harassment, though, we see a different picture. Would we want companies using language that discourages reporting of sexual harassment? Would we want the police using the word *tattling* to discourage people from reporting hate crimes? Because most targets of bullying cannot solve the problem themselves, we should not discourage them from telling. Because telling teachers when someone else is being hurt—an act that adults sometimes call "whistleblowing"—is behavior we want to encourage, we should not use language that discourages students from doing so.

Adult practices that discourage telling.

Since writing the first edition of this book, I have found another strategy to deal with students' truly unimportant complaints. Why would students tell us that someone has three pencils, that someone is burping, or that someone has her shoes untied? As I see it, the most common motivation for that kind of "tattling" behavior is a wish to get adult attention. If we respond to that "tattling" statement by giving on-the-spot instruction in the difference between telling and tattling, we have reinforced the tattling behavior. I have had greater success with a different intervention. I tell students at the beginning of the year that I want to hear about their concerns. I tell them that I will not *take action* about everything they report to me, because some things are not against the school rules. I also tell them that interrupting me while I am teaching will lead to consequences unless there is clearly an emergency. Then, when a student tells me about something unimportant, I can smile, thank the student for telling me, and move on to the task at hand. The "tattling" student gets less attention, the lesson can continue uninterrupted, and I can still take comfort in knowing that I have assured the students that I encourage them to report their concerns.

We can also encourage young people to reach out in friendship to bullied and isolated youth so that everyone is included. Goleman (1995), in his book *Emotional Intelligence,* states the importance of including all students in peer culture:

> How popular a child was in third grade has shown
> to be a better predictor of mental health problems
> at age 18 than anything else—teachers' and nurses'
> ratings, school performance and IQ, even scores
> on psychological tests. (p. 251)

I wrote earlier about the teacher who found that his students began including a peer in their social circle when he modeled that inclusion for them. Our behavior toward young people who are socially awkward or different in some way sends a strong message.

There are more direct steps we can take to help young people feel included and liked. For example, we can ask popular and secure students to reach out to isolated peers. One form of reaching out was invented by a student at the Bean school and has since been used successfully in schools around the country. Jim was new to our school in the fourth grade. He came to see me in the counseling office in November to tell me that he had few friends. My first reaction was to ask him to wait. We are a small rural school. In many small schools friendship patterns are set in the early grades and new students often find few open slots for friendship. As a result, it can take a long time for new students to feel accepted.

Friendship teams.

Before I could explain this to Jim, he said, "I think I need a friendship team." I asked him what a friendship team does, and he told me, "They help me make friends. You can help them figure out how to do that." I asked him if he had specific students in mind, and he named four boys in his grade who were both well liked and kind and who I knew would be interested. All six of us met at lunch the next day and worked out three roles for the friendship team members:

1. They would invite Jim to participate in games and activities so he wouldn't always have to ask to be included.
2. They would say nice things about him to other students.
3. If Jim did something that would prevent other children from being friends with him, friendship team members would let Jim know in a kind way, and he would listen.

We subsequently met four times to review what each had done to help. Jim identified what the others had done each week and thanked them for their help. At the end of the fourth meeting he told us all that he had made friends and that our work was done. Jim continues to be a well-respected and popular student at our school. This model has worked well with other students at many schools. I have learned that with students who are isolated and have relatively good social skills, three or four brief meetings are enough. Students who are difficult to make friends with because of mood disorders or social skills deficiencies may need an ongoing effort, and the members of their friendship teams may need more training and support. In helping schools implement friendship teams, I have learned that middle school students are unlikely to ask adults for help in making friends. In grades 5 and higher, we can instead train and support small groups of concerned students as friendship teams at large. These students actively search for isolated peers and invite them into activities, ask them to sit with the group at lunch, and attempt to include them in other ways. It is also helpful to train these team members to allow isolated students to be alone, if those students choose to.

As in this example of friendship teams, bystander interventions can focus on training and supporting a selected group of student volunteers to help alienated or victimized students. Vaillancourt, Hymel, and McDougall (2003) write, "[W]hen bystanders do intervene on behalf of the victim, such behavior is typically only undertaken by students with high social status (e.g., Samilvalli, Lagerpetz, Bjorkqvist, Osterman, & Kaukiainen, 1996). If only high-status peers are likely to be successful in intervening on the part of the victim, perhaps they should be targeted in school-based intervention efforts." One project that involved recruiting and training high-status bystanders is the "School Watch" program, documented in Ross (1996, pp. 125–126). In this program, high school students were selected and trained to keep staff informed about bullying and other behaviors of concern at their school. Safeguards inherent in the program protected these School Watch members from retaliation. The parallel between this intervention and the United States National Sherriff's Association "Neighborhood Watch" program will help us to involve caring, high-status youth effectively in bullying prevention.

As we build a culture in which students expect that everyone will have friends, young people reach out spontaneously. By encouraging young people to pass on a positive school culture to younger and new students, we help students create durable change in their interactions with one another. Students begin to find their own ways of furthering the ideas of inclusion, fairness, and protection from harassment. As my daughter, Julia, pointed out to me years ago, when we teach young people that reaching out to friendless peers is in their own self-interest—that by reaching out, they get great friendships in exchange—we create a school culture where inclusion is spontaneous.

Our main goal should be a school culture in which every young person has friends, in which anyone who is harassed gets support, and in which problems are solved in nonviolent ways. There will always be conflicts, and there will always be young people who try to bully others. What we want to do is to create a peer culture in which students who bully will hear from peers: "We don't hurt other people here."

Suggested Reading for This Chapter and Chapter 17

Aronson (2000) and Brendtro, Brokenleg, and Van Bockern (1990) are good resources for strategies for building community, involving students in the life of the school, and creating interdependence. Rohd (1998) and Koppett (2001) present theater techniques to help us help peers educate one another. Curricula by Friedman (1996), Mullin-Rindler (2003), and O'Neill and Glass (2000) help us teach skills. Wessler (2003) presents clear, practical strategies for teaching and insisting on respect among students.

The fiction of Trudy Ludwig, Eve Bunting, Kate DiCamillo, Katherine Paterson, Russell and Lilian Hoban, Amy Goldman Koss, and Eleanor Estes helps us talk about complex issues with children.

Let's Get Real, by Debra Chasnoff (2004), is a wonderful video full of the authentic words and thoughts of real middle school students—targets, bullies, and bystanders. It offers a good focus on teacher and bystander action and is highly recommended for teacher training.

The Bully Busters curriculum is a clear, research-based, and helpful curriculum, mixed with excellent recommendations for teacher action; this curriculum comes in two books, one for grades K–5 (Horne, Bartolomucci, & Newman-Carlson, 2003) and the other for grades 6–8 (Newman-Carlson, Horne, & Bartolomucci, 2000).

Say Something, a book by Peggy Moss (2005), sends us three very important messages:

1. We stand up for others because we will all need people to stand up for us some day.
2. Bystanders' silence hurts targets of bullying.
3. When we reach out to other kids who are excluded, we make good friends.

CHAPTER 17

WHOLE-SCHOOL
EDUCATIONAL APPROACHES

We don't expect students to learn algebra on their own, or to become good violinists or competent tennis players without instruction. Yet somehow we think children can learn how to get along with each other merely by being thrown together at school. Some do . . . but many more students would get along if schools made human relations part of the curriculum. There are many ways to do this, from teaching children to recognize and understand their emotions, to helping students develop greater empathy for others, to giving students the tools to resolve conflicts, to actively teaching students the skills to make friends.

—Elliot Aronson (2000)

There is much schools can do to help young people develop prosocial behavior. When we look at what young people tell us about how they solve problems, we see that incidents of physical violence at school are related to assumptions about conflict that are held by many students. A recent report of student surveys helps us see this issue more clearly. The Josephson Institute's 2000 study summarizes interviews with over 15,000 students in schools spanning the United States. Seventy-five percent of high school boys and 60 percent of high school girls surveyed said they had hit someone in the past 12 months *because they were angry.* Forty-three percent of the boys and 19 percent of the girls said that it is OK to hit or threaten others when *others make them angry.* Thirty-nine percent of the middle schoolers and 36 percent of the high schoolers surveyed reported feeling unsafe at school, and 20 percent reported having brought a gun to school for self-protection in the past year.

> Seventy-five percent of high school boys and 60 percent of high school girls said they had hit someone in the past 12 months.

The students surveyed in this study help us see why we should educate youth in nonviolent conflict resolution. The words of the students show us that they have fundamental misunderstandings about the links between emotion and behavior. When these youth tell us that others "make them angry" or that they act violently "because they are angry," they show us that they have not learned to understand the roots of their own emotions or to make conscious behavioral choices. The language these students use parallels the way spouse abusers talk about their behavior. They, too, describe their targets as *making* them angry. They, too, avoid responsibility for their own actions by describing aggression as an inevitable result of other people's behavior toward them: "I hit her because she insulted me." In our efforts to combat these lines of reasoning, we have much to work against. Students learn that violence is justified from many sources, including violent TV and movies, their own parents or relatives, and their peers.

In the quote at the beginning of this chapter, Aronson identifies key goals for schools, including teaching children about emotion, building empathy, teaching skills for solving problems, and helping youth make friends. We can work toward these goals through classes taught by the guidance counselor or by teachers, peer-led seminars, and monthly school or grade-level assemblies. We can reinforce this instructional work when all staff model, prompt, and reinforce the skills we teach. At the James Bean School I teach 12-week classes in each grade level, starting with the basics of recognizing emotions and solving problems without hurting. As students get older, we move into learning skills to solve more complex problems, setting and attaining goals, and standing up for others. We hold monthly assemblies by grade to celebrate the school's successes, recognize acts of generosity and friendship, and discuss ways students and teachers can make the school a better place. We encourage older students to teach younger students about inclusion, conflict resolution, and generosity through helping them create short educational videos that we use at our monthly assemblies. Staff schoolwide reinforce skills through discussion.

> Teaching children about emotion, building empathy, teaching skills for problem solving, and helping youth make friends.

Elliot Aronson, in his 2000 book, *Nobody Left to Hate: Teaching Compassion after Columbine,* outlines steps to build compassionate schools. He urges us to:

- Teach emotional literacy.
- Build empathy.
- Increase appreciation for diversity.
- Help young people develop nonviolent conflict resolution techniques.
- Limit unfair competition, while encouraging cooperation.

Emotional literacy is the ability to express and understand our own emotions and the emotions of others. When we can understand our own anger and disappointment, we can learn to deal with these emotions in positive ways.

When we talk with first and second graders about emotions, we can teach them about how emotions feel and what they look like. Children can learn what to do when they feel sad or angry or scared. They can learn to identify these feelings in others and to support others who feel sad or angry or scared. Adolescents can learn about emotions on a deeper level. They can learn that anger is often a secondary emotion that obscures primary emotions of shame, inadequacy, or fear. That knowledge can help them to react more effectively to threatening or embarrassing situations.

Emotional literacy is the first step toward learning empathy and understanding the effects of our own actions. Empathy and understanding others' points of view can be taught in structured classroom lessons, such as those in the Second Step program. We can also teach empathy through discussing children's literature, in discussions of day-to-day classroom events, and through providing opportunities for service.

We can teach empathy as we discuss children's literature by talking to students about the actions and emotions of characters in a book. Literature offers students a chance to put themselves into

| Teaching empathy via children's literature. | other people's lives, act out scenes, talk about how characters feel, and explore alternative endings to stories. There are many useful books that help youth understand bullying, feelings, and friendship. A partial list of books I have used |

productively in classroom discussions includes the following: Eleanor Estes's *The Hundred Dresses;* Dr. Seuss's *Horton Hatches a Who;* Katherine Paterson's *The Great Gilly Hopkins* and *Bridge to Terabithia;* Kate DiCamillo's *Because of Winn-Dixie;* William Steig's *Brave Irene;* Russell and Lillian

Hoban's *Best Friends for Frances;* James Garfield's *Follow My Leader;* and many of Eve Bunting's books. Margy Burns Knight's excellent books are also indispensable.

You will have favorite books of your own. We can use these books by talking about how the different characters feel, what choices they face, why they decide on a course of action, and how we feel about them. We can act out scenes from the books, explore what different outcomes would result from different choices by the characters, and create different endings for the story.

Literature draws young people in because they care about the characters and about what happens to them so they can explore and learn from those characters' feelings and actions.

Empathy can be taught in the moment—at the time when a student's behavior has hurt someone else. As I discussed in chapter 12, instead of telling students why their behavior is wrong or asking the closed question "Did you hurt him?" we can ask, "What was wrong with what you did?" "Why do we have a rule against name-calling?" and "How can you tell you hurt her?" These questions are often more helpful than the common question, "How would you feel if someone called you that name?" After all, some students might not mind. Our work with aggressive youth is most powerful when we discuss their behavior using the same language and interpersonal problem-solving concepts that they have learned in classroom lessons (Shure, 2001d).

Finally, empathy can be taught by providing opportunities for generosity and public service, especially when that service is designed to help students learn about the needs and lives of others less fortunate than themselves. We help students build empathy when we involve them in acts of generosity ranging from peer tutoring to volunteering in a soup kitchen to helping rebuild homes. Community service projects can start with the youngest children, who can save

Public service.

pennies for the food bank or clean up the playground. Older elementary-grade students can tutor or read to younger ones, help teachers, assist the custodian, plan a food drive, or wash tables and help the kindergarten students pick up their forks and spoons at lunch. In middle schools and high schools, students have even larger opportunities to give back to their communities. In *Reclaiming Youth at Risk* (1990), Brendtro, Brokenleg, and Van Bockern write, "Without opportunities to give to others, young people do not develop as caring persons" (p. 50).

In addition, we can teach students to appreciate diversity as a source of joy and as enriching their lives and friendships. We all benefit as we move from tolerating diversity to delighting in it. As young people appreciate others for their differences, instead of in spite of their differences, the bullies' arguments that their targets "deserve it" begin to fall through. When young people form connections with a wide range of peers, they will be more likely to stand up for their peers when they are bullied.

We should teach conflict resolution techniques and support students when they use these skills. Note that bullying is harassment rather than conflict and that conflict resolution training will often not help targets stop bullying. Unresolved peer conflict, though, will often escalate into more serious nonbullying aggression. There are many effective curricula for teaching conflict resolution. I am most familiar with the Peacemaking Skills for Little Kids program (Friedman, 1996) and the Kelso's Choice program (O'Neill & Glass, 2000), and have seen good results from both. Remember that all of these curricula will work best in an environment where adults model and prompt the behaviors and attitudes being taught in their day-to-day interactions with students and colleagues. The Kelso's Choice program helps students differentiate between big problems for which students need adult help and small problems that students can solve by their own actions. The program then teaches nine methods for resolving or defusing conflict. Students practice each method, and teachers and other staff acknowledge students when they see them using Kelso's methods. If students try two methods to resolve a small problem and neither works, the program directs them to ask an adult for help.

We can also teach skills for standing up for others, solving problems without hurting, and building positive friendships through interactive theater. When students see and interact with a scenario, they are more likely to understand the feelings of the characters than if they just talk about it. When young people have the responsibility for creating solutions to a problem, they are more likely to think about what to do than when we tell them the right answer. Interactive theater allows us to create scenarios, check with students for the accuracy of the scenarios, challenge students to come up with solutions, and test the solutions in the context of the theatrical experience. We can then encourage young people to write about their learning and make a commitment to action. Age-appropriate use of interactive theater allows us to create opportunities for practice, involve students in generating solutions to real-life problems, and develop increased understanding about how others feel. Techniques drawn from improvisational theater also have the potential for making our discussions have greater emotional impact. Michael Rohd (1998) and Kat Koppett (2001) provide useful guides for utilizing interactive theater. The following quote, which has been attributed to many sources, most notably Confucius, communicates best why interactive and improvisational theater are so helpful in helping young people change: "Tell me and I forget; show me and I remember; involve me and I understand."

Finally, we can limit unfair competition, where some students have more chance of succeeding than others. We can structure cooperation toward common goals. The social psychologist Muzafer Sharif designed an experiment to see how easy it would be to create an atmosphere of intense animosity between groups of young people and how easy it would be to heal that animosity. In Sharif's study, which is described in Aronson's 2000 work, youngsters were assigned randomly to one of two groups when arriving at summer camp. Researchers set up a series of competitive activities that led to closeness within each group and a sense of distance and rivalry between the groups. They intensified the rivalry by creating situations in which one group was treated better than the other group. For example, one of the groups was invited to arrive at a camp party earlier than the other group. At the party there were both fresh and appealing treats and food that was stale and squashed. The first group to arrive ate all of the good food. When the second group arrived and learned what had happened, they began harassing the first group. The first group responded in kind, and name-calling escalated into a food fight and riot. Sharif and his colleagues found the rivalry and hatred that developed between the two groups difficult to change, even after the experiment was over. Just eliminating the factors that had caused the rivalry did not reduce the tension. Even "when the two groups were engaged in such benign activities as watching movies, trouble was likely to break out" (Aronson, 2000, p. 121). However, the researchers did find a way to reduce intergroup hostility through creating situations in which youth from both groups had to work together to accomplish a common goal. As the young people were involved in a number of activities in which they all needed to work together for the common good, they began getting along.

Elliot Aronson (2000) ties these research results to what we do in schools in this way:

> Hostility between groups can form and become entrenched very easily. Signs of favoritism toward one group and other types of perceived unfairness can increase intergroup antagonism. If schools want to decrease the animosity among cliques, repressing it is not enough. Schools have to offer students a common goal that they can all work toward together, within a structure that supports a positive sense of belonging. (p. 119)

My first reaction in reviewing Sharif's research was to shake my head in sadness, secure that most modern schools do nothing to create this type of antagonism. Then I started to think about the amount of money and time high schools often spend on programs for athletically or academically gifted students. Who can be chosen for the school teams? Who doesn't have a chance no matter how hard he or she tries? Who has the intellectual gifts to be on the honor roll?

If recognition and reward are available only to the students with above-average abilities, we are structuring uneven competition. In addition, I thought of all the stories I have heard about "good" students being allowed to walk through schools unchallenged, while "bad" students were asked for their passes, or of some students being immune from consequences for their actions. In addition to ensuring fairness and equal access to resources and rewards, we should find ways to structure cooperation. As students work together to accomplish real tasks that make the school or the community a better place, they can break down barriers between groups. Finally, remember that observable adult behavior is the most powerful teaching tool we have. I have worked in schools where the staff modeled collegiality, inclusion, and friendly cooperation. I have also worked in schools where the staff formed cliques, talked about others behind their backs, competed with each other, and isolated colleagues. What will you do to assess and change negative models of staff-to-staff relationships? Young people are watching you. As the writer James Baldwin (1961) said, "Children have never been very good at listening to their elders, but they have never failed to imitate them."

Suggested Reading

See the end of chapter 16.

CHAPTER 18

PREVENTING DISABILITY HARASSMENT

Harassment is a form of discrimination. It reinforces hierarchies of prestige and peer acceptance within the school setting. School children with disabilities are significantly lower in social prestige than other students. . . . In any context, school or work, harassment frequently serves to reinforce lessons about who is in the accepted group and who is in the out group. Vicki Schultz has observed how even sexual harassment is often not at all sexual. It consists instead of constant reinforcement of the message that the woman does not belong in the position she occupies. Similarly, disability harassment constantly reinforces the message that the child with disabilities does not belong and that nothing he or she does can change that reality.

—Mark Weber (2002)

After I published the first edition of this book, I began hearing from parents and advocates, asking me to add material about disability harassment. They told me about young people who are teased, excluded, threatened, and hit. In writing this chapter I want also to honor the many teachers I have known who have cared deeply about their students who had disabilities and who have worked successfully to meet the needs of all students in their classes. And I have known many students who have been great friends of and advocates for peers with disabilities. This chapter is about what can go wrong and what we can do about it.

I write this chapter knowing that the word *disabilities* covers a wide range of conditions. Most of the students with disabilities whom I have known are resilient, kind people who are well accepted by their peers. In some parts of this chapter I will write about disabilities that affect students' thinking, their behavior toward others, and their vulnerability to bullying.

Weber's article, cited at the beginning, discusses three categories of disability harassment:

> First, outright physical mistreatment and verbal abuse of highly vulnerable children by school personnel; second, conduct by teachers that treats children with disabilities unfairly and actively encourages fellow students to join in the ridicule; and third, failure to provide protection against known risks of physical or psychological harm by other students, often including the risk of physical assault. (Weber, p. 1085)

Meredith Warshaw, who runs the informative Web site http://www.uniquelygifted.org, described some types of harassment of youth with Asperger's syndrome, obsessive-compulsive disorder, and similar conditions, in an e-mail:

Young people who have some disabilities may act, dress, or look different from peers. Sometimes peers harass them about these differences. Some young people with disabilities are easy to provoke into behavior that will get them punished. Peers can harass them by provoking that behavior and so getting them in trouble. Some students often don't understand social rules, and peers may take advantage of that by setting them up to do inappropriate things. (Warshaw, personal communication, May 13, 2004)

A brief search of news accounts and articles yielded these examples:

Robert was a seventh grader with an undiagnosed visual impairment. His teacher routinely called him "butthead" and said she would like to take out his eyes and give them to a child who would work harder. His mother complained to Robert's principal and ultimately to the Board of Education. After the principal assured Robert's mother that the teacher would apologize if necessary, the teacher called Robert up to the front of the class, got down on her knees and in an exaggerated voice said, "I'm so sorry, Bobby!" She then turned to the class and stuck a finger in her throat to mimic inducing vomiting. At some point the next year, after the visual impairment was diagnosed, Robert was moved to another teacher's room. (Weber, p. 1085)

Shawn was a 10-year-old with Tourette's syndrome. . . .When Shawn made involuntary body movements due to tics, the teacher and aides tackled and sat on him. . . . At times, Shawn was punished for failing to perform tasks by being deprived of meals or having water sprayed on his face. The teacher screamed degrading remarks at Shawn. Shawn was also forced to write the sentences "I will not tell my mom" and "I will not tic." He was threatened with physical harm if he ever told his mother about what was happening at school. (Weber, p. 1085)

Several students continually remark out loud to other students during class that a student with dyslexia is "retarded" or "deaf and dumb," and does not belong in the class; as a result, the harassed student has difficulty doing work in class and her grades decline. . . .

A student repeatedly places classroom furniture or other objects in the path of classmates who use wheelchairs, impeding the classmates' ability to enter the classroom. . . .

A professor repeatedly belittles and criticizes a student with a disability for using accommodations in class, with the result that the student is so discouraged that she has great difficulty performing in class and learning. . . .

Students continually taunt or belittle a student with mental retardation by mocking and intimidating him so he does not participate in class. (U.S. Department of Education, 2000)

With their video camera rolling, five teenagers beat, kicked and laughed at a special education student as he waited at a bus stop, police said. Then, they said, the attackers "laughed hysterically" as they sped away. (Plohetski, 2003)

Three Green Bay teens were convicted Monday of beating up a 15-year-old disabled classmate in

October. . . . According to the criminal complaint,
the boys chased the victim—who was riding a bicy-
cle— . . . down Seventh Street. The suspects rode
in a minivan as the victim pedaled west. . . . [T]he
suspects hit the victim's bike with the minivan.
The older boys held the victim on the ground,
kicked him and spit on him and choked him with
his shirt. At one point, [one of them] asked the victim, "How does a steel toe feel?" and then stomped
on the victim's head. The victim, who is now 16,
did not appear in court. His parents were present
for Monday's hearing. The victim's mother said
he suffers from high-functioning autism. (Nelesen,
2003)

How can these things happen? One clue to what makes this
behavior possible can be found in the statement of one of those
Green Bay teens. In the same newspaper article he is reported to
have said that he felt sorry for his actions. He said he realized that
he had been "stupid and childish." Young people who minimize
their actions, who describe kicking someone in the head as "childish" instead of acknowledging the brutality of that behavior, have
not learned to take full responsibility for their actions. Instead they
have learned the value of a quick and superficial apology. Yet the
roots of disability harassment lie deeper than the failure of one individual teen to develop a fully working conscience. The experience
and status of young people with disabilities in this country seem to
me to parallel the experiences of other groups.

Since my childhood, the United States has initiated two major
efforts to integrate excluded or marginalized groups of people with
disabilities into the mainstream: deinstitutionalization of people
with serious mental illness and mainstreaming of children with disabilities into regular public school classrooms. In each case the
goals included improving the life opportunities of the group being

included and helping the culture develop more positive, accepting attitudes.

Growing up in the excellent schools of Brookline, Massachusetts, in the 1950s, I do not remember a single classmate with a disability. I do remember seeing some students getting off the bus and going into a building we called "manual training." I think that my town's young people with disabilities must have gone to that other school instead. We never met them. When I was 10 years old, I read John Garfield's wonderful book about blindness, *Follow My Leader* (1957). I never questioned where the blind children were in my community. If I had, I would have assumed that they went to a special school somewhere else.

My classmates and I had no opportunity to make friends with or to harass these young people. Our teachers had no opportunity to teach them or to be impatient with them. These students had their own separate world: in many ways a limited and limiting one. Now almost all young people who have disabilities are in the mainstream. Most of them benefit greatly from the opportunities and the membership in the wider world that comes with mainstreaming. Many are in schools that provide them with safe, nurturing environments in which to learn. Some, though, are harassed. When schools cut budgets, educating young people with disabilities is sometimes seen as the reason that there is not enough money for other programs. When money is tight and young people with disabilities are in classrooms with inadequate support, those students are sometimes resented. People believe that their needs or their behavior interferes with others' learning. Sometimes young people with disabilities are resented for having rights and protections that other children do not have, as though they and their parents have chosen their disabilities to get unfair protections. In the absence of vigorous action to combat these perceptions and to protect these young people from harassment, our culture builds the attitudes that make events like the beating in Green Bay possible.

There are strong parallels between mainstreaming and deinstitutionalization of people who are mentally ill. I began my career in mental health in 1969 at a state psychiatric hospital in Denver. Many of the residents of the adult division were in the hospital involuntarily. Some were hospitalized involuntarily because they had harmed others or were at risk for harming others. Yet some of our patients were hospitalized involuntarily only because they had been judged to be incapable of caring for themselves. Psychiatric hospitals in those days carried the legacy of the "asylum" or "place of safety," as well as being places for mental health treatment.

When I moved to Maine in 1972, I saw the first waves of deinstitutionalization and the birth of community mental health centers. People with severe mental illness were to have the freedom to live their own lives in their communities within a network of support. They were to be protected and to have access to services. In some places that supportive network helped many people make the transition to independent living and true freedom. In too many other places, deinstitutionalization became a way to save money. People were "free" to move from hospitals to the street, to shelters, or to jail. In many communities the supportive network of services that was supposed to help people make the transition to independent living never materialized. Even now, 35 years later, homeless people with severe mental illnesses are frequent targets of brutal harassment.

Integrating people who have significant differences or who are unusually vulnerable to the effects of harassment into a general population requires that we take extra steps to support them and to protect them from harassment. It requires money and other resources. And if we are in the front lines and experience these realities without those resources, it is sometimes hard not to blame the people with disabilities for the extra work they bring us. Self-awareness and self-monitoring are important as we help and protect these people.

Dealing with harassment of vulnerable students

Some young people are more vulnerable to bullying than others. Some of those vulnerable students have been diagnosed with disabilities; some have not. Other students may be experiencing painful parental divorce, acute physical illness, or other situations that make "minor" harassment overwhelming. Our goal in working with vulnerable students should be fourfold: (a) to model acceptance and respect, (b) to help them succeed in positive social interactions with peers, (c) to protect them from harassment, and (d) to help them become more resilient.

Staff attitudes and modeling

As with every other type of bullying, the adults in the school play the primary roles in preventing harassment through modeling. When adults welcome and include young people with disabilities, students see that. When adults set and follow through on expectations that students with disabilities will be treated with respect, the student body learns to behave respectfully. I have worked in many schools where I see adults taking the lead in both these areas. Talking with young people to build awareness of the needs of youth with disabilities is important but is likely to be effective only in the context of positive modeling and clear expectations from adults. Our own attitudes toward young people with disabilities will have the strongest influence on the attitudes of their peers.

Young people are always watching the adults in their lives. How do we feel about having youth with disabilities in our classrooms? In our schools? When we have national policies that say that teachers and schools have failed if any students do not learn everything listed in the state curriculum standards, how do we welcome youth with significant disabilities? What are we to do if inadequate supports for the needs of these young people mean that we leave work at the end of the day exhausted or with a feeling of having cheated our other students to meet the needs of a few? These are not simple questions to answer. Our own self-awareness and our ability to move past our frustrations to actively welcoming every student are key elements in creating safe schools. As colleagues, supervisors, and support staff, we have a responsibility to listen for the telltale signs of anger and frustration being directed at a student and to help each other welcome and affirm all our students. Staff discussions on these issues can help. One excellent training tool for staff is "How Difficult Can This Be? The F.A.T. City Workshop" (Lavoie, 1989), designed to help us remember the struggles that young people with disabilities go through in learning.

Training and support for teachers is important in helping staff see the invisible disabilities—those learning disabilities that are sometimes hard to diagnose or that show themselves later than other difficulties. Young people with these disabilities can look to us like bright children who aren't trying. For example, I have found that it is especially easy for teachers to become frustrated and angry with students with undiagnosed written expression disorder (dysgraphia). Independent written expression is ". . . the ultimate, most complex method of expression. It involves infinitely complex multiple brain mechanisms, highly synchronized processing and has multiple sources and locations for the disruption of activity" (Kay, 2004). Students with dysgraphia may appear bright and capable in conversation—and then produce very primitive written work. "I know he can do the work," teachers tell me, "because he tells me the answer to the question. Then when I walk away to help another student, he just sits there and doesn't write it down." I have learned to say, "We only know students can do something when we have seen them do it."

In building positive staff attitudes, it is important to find the right balance between inclusion and specialized instruction. We need to balance between the professional responsibilities of educators and their needs for support as they work with challenging students.

I remember an experience that showed me what can happen if we use mainstreaming without supports. I attended a conference about inclusion in which a case study was presented. The conference organizers described a "success story" in which an aggressive student with disabilities was fully integrated into a regular classroom with minimal supports from special education. This student continued to hurt other students on a regular basis. The teacher led frequent meetings to help the other students learn how they could avoid getting this student angry. I got the impression that the teacher and the students spent their days walking on eggshells to keep this student calm so they could be safe and learn. Sometimes the *unsupported* inclusion of a student with behavioral disabilities disrupts the education of the majority and puts that majority at risk of harm. When this is true, it is difficult for any teacher to remain welcoming and positive toward that student. It is important to have adequate supports, consequences, rewards, and expectations for aggressive young people with disabilities so both they and their peers can be safe and educated.

Building an inclusive school culture is an important part of changing the behavior of individual staff. I remember a day a few years ago when I had been running all day between crises with individual students and families and classroom guidance meetings. As educators so often do, I had worked through lunch. I was tired. In my last class of the day, a student I knew who had fetal alcohol syndrome had interrupted me and his peers continuously. When I asked him to leave the circle and sit at his desk, he started yelling and wouldn't calm down. After school I went into the teachers' room and complained about having to teach kids with FAS. I talked about how much more I could have accomplished if he wasn't there. The other teachers in the room could have agreed with me that we shouldn't be expected to put up with students with disabilities. Instead they gently reminded me that that student also needed to learn the lessons I was teaching. I realized that part of what had gone wrong was that my irritation about "having to" teach him had contributed to his disruptive behavior. I found other ways to work with him in future class sessions.

How else can schools show that we value all youth?

One example comes to mind. I consulted with a junior high school in Missouri with a unique reward program for students. At the end of each year, students could earn a trip to one of the nearby cities with their class. Students earned the trip by getting 25 points throughout the year. Points could be earned in many different ways. They got points by earning high grades, by maintaining good behavior, by playing sports, by entering an art show, by performing school or community service, by getting their parents to attend evening meetings, and in many other ways. The principal told me that more than 90 percent of the students earned the trip every year. This is an example of a system in which every student can earn positive recognition. It is unlike recognition just for the honor roll or just for varsity sports, where not every student has the opportunity to earn the reward. When every student can be recognized for real effort or real contributions to the school community, we give the message that all students belong.

Language and assumptions

Bullying is caused by the bully, not by the target. It is important that we become aware of our internal language and assumptions. When we say: "Kenny gets teased because he has Asperger's syndrome," we are suggesting that disabilities naturally lead to harassment. This is not the case. There are schools where being different does not lead to being bullied. We can shift our internal and spoken language to: "Ken has Asperger's syndrome. Other students have been teasing him."

When adults or peers allow words that refer to young people's handicaps—like *retard, stupid sped, idiot,* or *dummy*—to be used in the school environment, we make harassment more possible. This is true even when those words are used to disparage events or objects. ("Those shoes are so retarded.") When we allow the use of this language, we allow ways of thinking that demean young people with disabilities.

How, then, can we talk about a student's limitations or differences in a respectful way? I remember a discussion I once had with a first-grade class about their classmate. He had autism and would scream when people talked with him or to make his needs known. The teacher and I asked what the students had observed and what they thought it meant. "He doesn't talk," they said. "I couldn't talk when I was a baby, and then I had to scream to get what I wanted." We asked what they thought would happen in the future. "He'll learn to talk," they said, "and then he won't need to scream anymore." This is exactly what happened. The students asked if they could move away from him if his screaming made it hard for them to do their work, and we discussed ways to do this in a pleasant way. We talked about how they could ask for help on the rare occasions when he took things, poked, or hit, and about how we would help them. They talked about having found ways to play with him. This kind of discussion is valuable because it helps young people build from observation through reflection to positive action and pride in that action.

Modeling and positive use of language are not all that are needed. Consistent, escalating consequences for peer aggression are also necessary for limiting harassment. We prevent harassment best when we hold each person involved responsible for his or her behavior. If a student tells a young person with Asperger's syndrome to grab another student's breasts, the student who instigated the behavior should earn a consequence and be expected to reflect on his or her behavior. That consequence should be greater than the consequence that would be earned for telling a student without a disability to grab another student's breasts. The student with Asperger's syndrome also needs to learn not to grab other students in private areas, even when someone else says to do so. He or she should also be accountable in a significant way for his or her actions. I have worked with two adults with physical disabilities who had very limited understanding of social relationships and how to work effectively with others. Both of these adults were clearly capable of learning how to get along with others. I believe, after working with them, that teachers, parents, supervisors, and peers had avoided telling them about the impact of their actions on others because of their disabilities. When we are aware that a person's actions alienate or hurt others, we do that person no favor by being silent.

Encouraging reporting and maintaining careful supervision

It is important to encourage children to tell staff when they have been bullied. Adults should make it clear by their actions that these reports will be taken seriously and acted upon. Young people with cognitive disabilities, or with disabilities that limit their understanding of interactions with others, will need very concrete and specific lessons in what to report and to whom. As in other training in social skills, attention should be paid to making sure that this learning transfers to real-life situations. We have a responsibility to ask questions and supervise interactions more closely when we are dealing with these vulnerable youth. When young people with limited communication skills show us through behavior change that they are in distress, we may have to ask more specifically about harassment or abuse by peers or adults.

When a student bullies a peer who is vulnerable because of disability or life situations, we should let the bullying student and his or her parents know that repeated harassing actions will lead to more serious consequences than usual. We can and should include disability, along with race, religion, and gender, in our list of types of harassment leading to more severe consequences. When the target has a disability, as defined by law, it is important to make bullying students aware that they are violating federal law and the civil rights of the target. We should then follow through to ensure that those rights are respected. After adults have followed through with enforcement, we can make other students aware of their responsibility to stand up for vulnerable targets. Winkie Mitchell, an Ohio guidance counselor, helps students to imagine that they have a younger brother or sister with a disability. Those students then have no trouble describing how they would want their sibling's classmates to behave. Then they can focus more effectively on how they themselves should behave when they see harassment of vulnerable peers.

Consequences for aggressive students with disabilities

It can be challenging to find effective consequences for aggressive students with some disabilities. Even when there is a schoolwide discipline rubric for aggressive behavior, some students will have their own systems of positive and negative consequences. Yet all students need to be held to expectations that they not hurt others. We do not help young people when we assume that they cannot control themselves, as they may grow up with that belief. When students with disabilities have reacted aggressively to teasing or hitting, we should hold them responsible for the choices they made at the same time as we hold the provoking student responsible for the provocation. What other choices did the vulnerable student have? Only when there was truly no other choice should we give all the responsibility to the provoking student. We help all students best when we both protect them from harassment and teach them how to deal with difficult situations without hurting others.

Reducing students' vulnerability to bullying through building resiliency and stress management skills

As I described in the chapter about supporting targets, it is often useful to teach relaxation techniques, to encourage vulnerable students to stay in the present instead of thinking about bullying as something that "always happens," and to understand that other students' bullying behavior is not the target's fault. Students with different disabilities will benefit from different interventions to help them learn to respond calmly, nonaggressively, and assertively to bullying. Often, successful interventions will be based on real-world examples, will involve repeated practice to mastery, and will be presented in or near the real situation. If we want a student to learn to respond calmly on the playground, our practice sessions should happen on the playground.

The techniques taught sometimes need to be very specific. For some students, it is important that all adults at school and home use the same words in talking about bullying. A young person who is easily provoked to hit others may need a short slogan to say to herself. Some such slogans are: "I will keep my hands and feet to myself." "Hands are not for hitting." "When someone says to hit, I should tell." "When someone calls me stupid, I should get away and tell." The student may need a visual cue for these actions, like a cartoon or a symbol showing the desired action. An end-of-day reflection time and reward might focus on the desired behavior and on the student's successes in self-control. One question I have found useful is "Tell me about a time today you almost hit someone." Another is "Tell me about a good choice and a bad choice you made today." What we should avoid is "I had a good day," "I was good," "I was bad." We help young people change their behavior when we help them focus on actions and choices.

Mark Haddon's wonderful novel, *The Curious Incident of the Dog in the Night-Time* (2004), presents clearly the need for clear, concrete instructions and a focus on specific actions for some students. His narrator, a young man with Asperger's syndrome, says:

> When people tell you what to do it is often confusing and does not make sense. For example, people often say "Be quiet," but they don't tell you how long to be quiet for. . . . Also I don't know what Father means when he says "Stay out of other peoples' business," because I do not know what he means by "other peoples' business" . . . Siobhan [the boy's teacher] understands. When she tells me not to do something, she tells me exactly what it is that I am not allowed to do. And I like this.

> For example, she once said, "You must never punch Sarah or hit her in any way, Christopher. Even if she hits you first. If she does hit you again, move away from her and stand still and count from 1 to 50, then come and tell me what she has done, or tell one of the other members of the staff what she has done."
>
> Or, for example, she once said, "If you want to go on the swings and there are already people on the swings, you must never push them off. You must ask them if you can have a go. And then you must wait until they have finished."
>
> But when other people tell you what you can't do they don't do it like this. So I decide for myself what I am going to do and what I am not going to do." (pp. 29–30)

Young people with sensory issues may need to leave a situation when their sensory input becomes overwhelming. I have found that many of these students can learn to tolerate more sensory input. They can learn to differentiate between gentle non-aggressive touch and being hit.

Helping students with disabilities develop friendships and find advocates

To help vulnerable young people make friends, we can work both to support their social skill development and to recruit peers who will reach out to them. After staff responses to harassment are in place, we can enlist peers to include, befriend, and stand up for young people with disabilities. Sometimes this inclusion takes the form of friendship teams. Three trained peers volunteer to invite an isolated student into activities. Sometimes peers will learn gentle ways to remind a student with a handicap about social expectations or about thinking before acting. Sometimes peers will model prosocial behaviors in a social skills group. Sometimes they will walk with or stand up for a vulnerable classmate. No matter which of these roles peers take, our appreciation is important. Most important, though, is their realization that they benefit by making good friends for themselves. I once asked a group of middle schoolers to tell me about a friend they value who is different from peers in some way. One student told us about a boy with Asperger's syndrome who had been her friend at her last school. "He was the best listener I've ever met," she said, "He wasn't always trying to figure out what he was going to say next."

We adults also can befriend isolated youth through sharing tasks, having fun with them, and showing interest in their lives. Every positive relationship isolated students have makes them more resilient and makes the next friendship easier.

A parent of a boy with Asperger's syndrome once asked me: "How do I talk about bullying with my child? Experiencing or seeing bullying bothers him." Many young people are bothered by bullying because it challenges their view of the world as a safe place. They want to believe that people can be trusted. Youth with autism spectrum disorders may be particularly sensitive to this issue. I would suggest telling the young person that some people are mean to others and discussing how to tell those people apart from others. Then we can talk about and practice specific strategies to avoid being with those people, seek protection from adults and peers, and make friends with people who are not mean.

Understanding and changing our reactions to differences

How do we overcome our reactions to differences—physical or behavioral? I remember Devon, the first student I ever worked with who had Asperger's syndrome. He would ask me over and over about jokes ("And how about this one—is this one funny?"). He would talk repetitively about dinosaurs and about his other somewhat obsessive interests. For some months I felt uneasy before, during, and after our meetings. The reciprocal rhythm I expected to find in conversations was lacking. I did not look forward to seeing him. Then I read Oliver Sacks's book *An Anthropologist on Mars: Seven Paradoxical Tales* (1996), which introduces us to the lives and thinking of people with Asperger's syndrome. I realized that if I looked at Devon as if he were an anthropologist *from* Mars, his behavior would make sense. His struggle to understand what humor is became the curiosity of a scientist. The unusual feel of communicating with him suddenly became a source of enjoyment rather than uneasiness. Similarly, I have seen teachers change their attitudes toward young people with Asperger's syndrome after reading *An Anthropologist on Mars,* Temple Grandin's autobiography, *Thinking in Pictures—and Other Reports from My Life with Autism* (1996), or Mark Haddon's novel *The Curious Incident of the Dog in the Night-Time* (2004). Books that help us see a disability from the inside can transform our reactions. There are many such books about different disabilities, and they are invaluable both for adults and students.

Miller and Sammons's (1999) book *Everybody's Different: Understanding and Changing Our Reactions to Disabilities* presents a useful series of learning strategies for adults and students. I recently had a chance to use some of their material with fourth graders. We began with a brainteaser about someone who was very short and thus kept winning a dance contest—the dance being the limbo. I talked about the very short teacher I met last year in my travels who told me that everyone he grew up with had treated him respectfully and included him. I asked the students what kinds of physical differences they see in people in their world. They described height, weight, mobility, skin color and racial differences, people who meet or don't meet cultural definitions of beauty, people who talk to themselves, and other differences they see and hear. I asked them how they feel when they see someone who is markedly different from the people they know. They talked about uneasiness, anxiety, and feeling "funny." We discussed our ability to let these feelings go when we realize that the other person is not a threat. Then they were ready to talk about what they think people with physical or behavioral differences want and need from them.

Our view of young people with disabilities can change as we experience their strengths. I have found, for example, that my chess program at school always has a high proportion of students who have Attention Deficit Disorder. Three of the past five years, a chess player with ADD has won our school chess championship. Some of these chess players with ADD play imaginatively, create unusual attacks, and focus intently on the 64-square chess board. When I read Thom Hartmann's book *Attention Deficit Disorder: A Different Perception* (1997), I was reminded of this observation. Sometimes disabilities bring strengths with them. Sometimes people with disabilities have marked strengths in areas not affected by the disability. As we see the whole person, not just the disability, we are able to make positive connections with that person.

Our goal in schools should not be tolerance. After all, we tolerate a headache. We tolerate bad food. We tolerate an uncomfortable bed. Our goal should be a school that actively welcomes all students.

> Disability harassment is preventable and cannot be tolerated. Schools, colleges, and universities should address the issue of disability harassment not just when but before incidents occur. . . . [A]wareness can be an important element in preventing harassment in the first place. The Department of Education is committed to working with schools, parents, disability advocacy organizations, and other interested parties to ensure that no student is ever subjected to such conduct. . . . When disability harassment limits or denies a student's ability to participate in or benefit from an educational institution's programs or

activities, the institution must respond effectively. Where the institution learns that disability harass-ment may have occurred, the institution must inves-tigate the incident(s) promptly and respond appropriately. (U.S. Department of Education, 2000)

Suggestions for Further Reading

http://www.bridges4kids.org and http://www.geocities.com/fishstep/harass.html are excellent resources for information and support. The Weber article and U.S. Department of Education let-ter cited in this chapter will help clarify legal issues related to dis-ability harassment. The Ohio Legal Rights Service has an excellent Web page for parents about advocating for the needs of students with disabilities, titled *What Can I Do If My Child with a Disability Is Being Harassed in School?*

CHAPTER 19

IMPLEMENTING A BULLYING PREVENTION PROGRAM

*In the end we will remember not the words of our enemies,
but the silence of our friends.*

—Martin Luther King Jr.

Dan Olweus's (2000) *Teacher Handbook: Olweus' Core Program against Bullying and Antisocial Behavior* presents detailed step-by-step guidance for program implementation. The following is my own brief list of recommended implementation strategies.

The first step is for a core of two or three people at a school who feel passionately about reducing bullying to educate themselves in what works and begin igniting enthusiasm in others. These champions of bullying prevention will be the key players in identifying existing practices that work or don't work and keeping the program energized and focused.

These two or three people can recruit and inspire four or five additional people. This larger group (which should include the principal, teachers, and counselors) will be the school's bullying prevention committee. The committee should begin by administering a student survey to help understand the dimensions of the problem and to focus the intervention. They also begin the work of identifying schoolwide behavior expectations, organizing consequences, and encouraging positive staff-student connections. At the same time, this group can identify and encourage existing positive practices by staff. Beginning by affirming the worth and effectiveness of those current practices that are working will lessen resistance to change. In the process of program design, the committee should search for simple procedures that will not make more work for already overwhelmed educators. I suggest being careful about one issue that often comes up in implementation. We should avoid discipline practices that punish the teacher who sees bullying by requiring extensive paperwork or investigation by the adult who reports. Similarly, we can be careful that reporting bullying does not give the reporter sole responsibility for supervising consequences. The more extra work comes along with witnessing and reporting bullying, the more likely staff are to look the other way.

The next step is training for the entire staff to help them discard myths, understand the school's role in preventing bullying, and use the discipline process. A few people should be trained in using the reflection form. The committee can help staff implement positive acknowledgment with students and with each other, as well as practices such as greeting, mentoring, extracurricular activities, notes home, and friendship teams. They can work to identify and build ways to protect staff-student time together.

The committee can then work with staff to create a discipline program that fits within the school's mission and culture. Students and parents should be involved throughout this process through educational meetings, newsletter articles, and the presence of representative parents on the committee. The school community will work for consensus on specific expectations, consequences, and a clear statement of who does what within the disciplinary practices.

When the school community understands the goals and has been trained in the practices of the intervention, implementation can begin, with a date set to review and revise the system. There will be a surge of discipline referrals for the first three to six weeks, as behavior that was not dealt with systematically in the past is reported more consistently. Subsequently, schools report dramatic decreases in reports of aggression as students understand that staff will continue to intervene.

The committee's work will continue as they monitor the program to ensure follow-through, look for ways to improve, and give feedback to staff, students, and families on successes. Positive feedback on success is the most powerful force for keeping the program going.

Suggested Reading

Olweus (2000) and Sharp and Smith (1994) are detailed and specific in their treatment of implementation. Mager and Pipe (1999) provide a clear view of ways in which administrators can help staff change student behaviors. Block (1999) describes methods for fostering change in a system when you do not have supervisory authority.

CHAPTER 20

TEN STEPS TO BUILDING SCHOOLS WHERE EVERYONE BELONGS

The most difficult part of all discipline is welcoming the student we wish wasn't there.

—Gerard Evanski (2004)

1. **Establish clearly defined schoolwide behavior expectations rather than rules that describe only general principles.**

Here is an example of a clearly defined rule: "No teasing. Teasing is name-calling, starting rumors, gestures, or other actions that are likely to make students feel bad about themselves." Here is a general principle: "We will treat each other with respect." Which of these rules will be more likely to lead to consistency among staff members in deciding whether a rule has been broken? General principles can be a guide in the creation of clearly defined expectations.

2. **Use predictable and escalating consequences for aggression rather than creating a unique consequence for each student and each situation.**

When there are inconsistent consequences for bullying, young people are likely to continue. When we have to customize a consequence for each incident, the process of discipline becomes impossibly time-consuming. Planned, rubric-based consequences take much less time to administer and thus can be used more consistently. When consequences are predictable and based on a clear rubric, young people can learn from each other's misdeeds. On the other hand, when two different students do exactly the same thing yet receive consequences of different severity, cause-and-effect learning is jeopardized. Students with more serious consequences, and their parents, are likely to believe that the consequence is unjust.

3. **Maintain a positive emotional tone between adults and youth rather than treating students with anger and frustration.**

When consequences come from a rubric, when they are earned rather than given, and when there are planned next steps if the student continues to choose aggression, there is no need for adults to use anger as a behavior management tool. When adults monitor their own feelings of frustration and look for small signs of progress, they are more able to develop positive relationships with at-risk youth. When adults model friendly and respectful communication, students are more likely to respond in kind.

4. Acknowledge positive actions rather than ignoring positive behavior or using person-based praise.

When staff point out students' positive behavior using descriptive language, students are more likely to repeat this behavior. We may say, "I noticed that you walked away instead of hitting when you were out in the game," "I saw you sit with Susan when she was alone at lunch," or "You complimented Bobby." When, in addition, we help students see the natural positive outcomes of their actions, we can be even more effective. We may say, "I noticed that you walked away instead of hitting when you were out in the game. You came back to the game and kept playing" or "I saw you sit with Susan when she was alone at lunch and I saw her smiling."

5. Provide structured opportunities for aggressive youth to think about their actions instead of using threats, lectures, or anger.

When young people take responsibility for their actions and for hurting others, they strengthen conscience. When they realize what goals they were trying to reach by being aggressive and find other ways to reach those goals, they learn to meet their needs in acceptable ways.

6. Work to develop a peer climate in which bystanders discourage bullying and in which peers befriend targets.

When 85 percent of the school population—the bystanders—stop watching silently and starts telling bullies to stop, telling adults, and reaching out in friendship, bullying behavior becomes less damaging and less frequent. The best way to encourage youth to make these changes is for adults to model the behaviors for them. We can set an example by implementing effective discipline systems, recognizing positive behaviors, and spending time listening to, sharing enjoyment with, and validating all students.

7. Protect targets and bystanders from repeated or retaliatory harassment.

Reducing the rate of bullying is the best support we can give targets. If we want young people to tell us about bullying, we have to make telling safe by using consequences for harassment of youth who report.

8. Help targets to reverse feelings of self-blame and to feel powerful.

"First they bully you, then you bully yourself," a student said to me in Florida. Targets often begin to believe what the bullies say about them: that they are stupid, ugly, or fat. Helping targets to see themselves more positively often takes time. They need to feel included and find ways to experience their strengths. As targets learn to brainstorm and apply problem-solving steps, they feel more competent.

9. Help targets build friendships.

Youth tell me that social isolation is the most painful part of being bullied. "If no one stands up for you, you feel like you don't exist," said one teenager in Ohio. We can encourage peers to reach out in friendship and help targets and other isolated youth participate in that friendship.

10. Recognize and build on the strengths and accomplishments of your school community.

When we recognize the positive programs and practices that stop bullying in a school, staff and students are more likely to continue them. When we track improvements and show everyone involved what they are doing to make a positive impact, it is more likely that people will stay committed to a bullying prevention program.

SUGGESTED ANSWERS FOR PRACTICE EXERCISES

Chapter 6

Exercise A

1. Statements A, B, C, and D are trait statements. They may be seen as insincere by students. Even if young people think we mean what we say, these statements encourage students to focus on their traits rather than on their actions.

   Statements F and G focus primarily on our emotional reaction to students. The student may learn to do good work to get approval, but may also choose to defy and frustrate us. Either way, the young person is developing extrinsic rather than intrinsic motivation.

   Statements E, H, and I are descriptive praise statements, which encourage students to examine their own behavior and see how they can make their own lives better.

2. Statements F and K are trait praise. They label children without telling them what they did to earn that label.

   Statements H and J focus on the adult's reaction to the behavior.

   Statements C, K, and L are not specific.

Statements A, B, D, E, G, and I are clear, descriptive feedback, which can help students see that they can make their own lives better.

Exercise B

1. The counselor, by identifying the positive results of Allie's actions, is pointing out a natural consequence of her actions.

2. By pointing out improvements in Jay's behavior and attributing those improvements to Jay's initiative to change, this teacher is acknowledging his behavior as part of a conscious effort to change.

3. By acknowledging how difficult it is to tell the truth when you've done something wrong, the principal is giving Ricky permission for pride.

4. As with Jay, the supervisor is acknowledging Margaret's self-control and attributing her behavior to a conscious effort to change.

5. By showing Jon how his behavior has a positive impact on his life, the teacher is pointing out a natural consequence of Jon's behavior.

Exercise C

1. Statement A incorporates acknowledgment of behavior in observable language with a statement of Bobby's apparent good intentions and attempts to improve his behavior. Statement D is also an effective acknowledgment statement, describing what Bobby did right. Both encourage internal motivation and empower Bobby to grow.

2. Statement B separates the aide's emotions from the praise and acknowledges Jean's initiative to change her behavior. Statement D is also effective because it both points out a specific action and shows the natural and observed consequences of that action.

3. Statements C, D, and E all acknowledge Cody's behavior in clear, observable language while separating his behavior from

adults' emotions. These brief statements about positive behavior observed by staff give Cody nothing to argue with and do not require that he care about adults' approval of his behavior. Over time, these statements help Cody see what he does right.

4. Statements B and C acknowledge the girls' behavior and show them the positive natural consequences of their actions.

5. Statements B and C show Brett the natural consequences of his actions, while acknowledging his behavior in observable terms. Statement D tells Brett what he did right. All three are helpful.

Chapter 12

1. We should accept answer G, which is free of excuses or minimizing and which states clearly what the young person did. All other answers need work.

2. Responses A, C, D, and E are all likely to work if they are said in a calm, moderately friendly tone of voice. We let students know that we will neither argue with them nor accept their denial.

3. Responses C and D are likely to work because they break the link between the student's behavior and the provocation.

4. Statements D and E can help young people drop the minimizing phrase "by accident." Some young people get stuck on this phrase. They may need you to help them discard it by acknowledging that they did not intend to hurt their target as much as they did. Remember to continue to hold them accountable for the actions they chose.

5. Statements F, G, H, J, and L are complete answers to the question. Students' nonverbal behavior will often guide you in deciding whether they are actually feeling empathy for their targets in addition to having a cognitive understanding of the impact of their behavior. If you sense little empathy, you can follow up by asking for more sensory details. What did the student see the other person do? What did the other person's face look like? What did the other person say?

6. Responses A and B, if said in a calm and patient tone of voice, can help focus students on their targets' reactions. Response D avoids a power struggle and often energizes the student to complete the task successfully. For this strategy to work, the statement should be made in a matter-of-fact way, with no attempt at threat or control, and be followed by the adult's moving away from the student to complete some other task.

7. Response B helps students drop the mental reservation implicit in the common phrases "might have" or "probably." Response C helps young people develop empathy and may be needed if response B does not work.

8. Response C helps young people understand the reasoning behind the school rules and thus move past externalization.

9. Response A helps students think about what they mean by these bland, evasive statements. Response B helps them focus on the results of their actions.

10. Response A may work, but B is more likely to be effective.

11. Response C will most likely be effective. We might also ask what goal the student was trying to reach, what the student wanted to happen next, or even what was happening before the action. The most important strategy is to offer three or four possible answers to the question rather than suggesting one.

12. The key to answering this question is to ask yourself which of the solutions has the potential to solve the specific problem the student is presenting. All of these solutions, except for B, C, D, and H (which do not describe actions) would work to solve some problems.

APPENDIX B

STOPPING BULLYING AND RAISING RESPONSIBLE, CARING CHILDREN: A HANDOUT FOR PARENTS

STOPPING BULLYING AND RAISING RESPONSIBLE, CARING CHILDREN: A HANDOUT FOR PARENTS

What is bullying? Hitting, name-calling, exclusion, or other behavior that is meant to hurt. Bullying is carried out by someone who has more power over someone who has less power.

Do we have to know that someone means to hurt someone else before we can discipline for behavior that hurts? No. When we discourage all peer-to-peer aggression, we also deal with bullying.

What are the effects of bullying? Bullying affects both targets and bullies. Targets of bullying are more likely to grow up depressed and anxious. Bullies are much more likely than nonbullies to become adult criminals.

Why not just tell kids to stand up for themselves or pretend it doesn't bother them? They've most likely already tried both of these interventions before asking us for help. If these strategies worked, they would already have solved the problem.

Bullying has much in common with sexual harassment, spousal abuse, and racism. There is an imbalance of power. The aggressor blames the target for causing or deserving the harassment. Targets often come to blame themselves.

What parenting styles lead to young people becoming (or not becoming) bullies? There are many other factors outside the family, but families where discipline is inconsistent and where there is little warmth and adult attention are more likely to raise children who bully. Consistent, fair discipline teaches self-control and responsibility. Warmth and time spent together teach connection and empathy.

From *Schools Where Everyone Belongs: Practical Strategies for Reducing Bullying* (2nd ed.) © 2007 by Stan Davis. Champaign, IL: Research Press (800-519-2707; www.researchpress.com).

What about factors outside the family? The more violent television, violent movies, violent video games, and music glorifying violence kids are exposed to, the more likely they are to solve problems in violent ways. We can limit kids' exposure to all these media.

What parenting style has the best results? Authoritative parents, who have clear rules and follow through on expectations and who show love and interest in the child's feelings, tend to raise the most confident, successful children. Authoritarian parents, who have clear (sometimes rigid) rules and who show little love or interest in their children, tend to raise children who either live by rules or rebel against them. Permissive parents, who give their children love and have inconsistent rules, tend to raise children who are confident and secure but who may have problems with self-control or with respecting the rights of others.

How can I set up a family discipline program that is consistent and effective? It's best to start with no more than five specific house rules that all the adults in the home agree are important and that apply to everyone. Some examples of house rules are "No hitting or teasing," "Do your homework and your chores on time," and "Follow directions after one reminder without screaming or whining."

Then make a list of all the privileges your children have, including TV, phone, rides, clothes of their choosing, video games, and other things you let them do or do for them. Take out of the list everything that has to be free for the child—those privileges, like sleeping in a bed or eating, that every child deserves no matter how he or she acts without having to earn them.

List the other privileges—at least 12—in order on the basis of how unhappy *you* would be if your child did not earn those privileges.

Now you are ready to begin. After you explain the rules and the behavior system, whenever your children break a house rule, they move down one level on the privilege chart. They can now have the privileges below that level but not the ones above. A laminated list of rules and an erasable marker are useful tools in making this chart clearer. For younger children (ages five to seven), allow them to earn back one level every two days according to their improved behavior. For young people ages eight and older, allow them to earn back one level each Friday on the basis of their improved behavior throughout the week. Privileges can be lost at any time but earned back only one at a time at these specified times. Avoid warning, threatening, begging, allowing second chances, arguing, or using anger. Instead, calmly let your child lose privileges every time he or she breaks a house rule. Remember to give lots of positive attention and spend time playing with, reading with, and enjoying your child whether he or she is misbehaving or not. Love does not have to be earned.

What about spending time with kids? The more time you spend with them doing things you both enjoy, the closer you will be to them and the happier they will be. Schedule special times for each child and stick to the schedule. Cut back activities, if necessary, to make that happen.

What kinds of praise work best? Praise is important. General, nonspecific praise like "You're so smart" or "Good job" doesn't help young people see what they did right and may make them afraid to risk failure if they think they can only be smart when they do something right. I-message praise, such as "I'm so proud of you when you . . . ." tells young people that they are responsible for our feelings and thus may lead to dependency or rebellion. Telling young people exactly what they did and what positive results their actions have empowers them and helps them learn to be proud of their own behavior: "I noticed you helped your brother get dressed for school. He was smiling after you did that." "You studied the last three nights, and you got a 95 on this test." "I saw you control yourself when Suzie yelled at you, and you stayed out of trouble."

What about bullying prevention programs in schools? Research-based bullying prevention programs combine six basic strategies schoolwide:

1. Clear expectations and consistent schoolwide consequences for hurting others with words or actions
2. Positive staff-student communication
3. Staff spending time with students
4. School staff helping aggressive youth change
5. Staff supporting targets of bullying
6. Staff helping bystanders discourage bullying

How can I talk with my child if she bullies someone else? Help your child tell you exactly what she did, without excuses or blaming others. Remember that even if the other student involved did something, your child made a choice to do what she did. Encourage her to talk about how that behavior affected the other person. Help her find the goal she was trying to reach through hurting the other person: Did she want attention? Power? Fun? To be left alone? And help her find other ways to reach that goal without hurting others. If your child has been punished at school, it will probably not be necessary to punish again at home (unless the behavior was severe). Encourage your child to act differently next time.

How can I support my child if he is bullied at school? Avoid blaming your child for the harassment. Think twice before giving advice—your child may have already tried the strategies you are going to suggest. Get as much information as you can. Talk with your child's teacher, principal, or counselor, and ask him or her to help your child be safe. That intervention may include consequences for the bully, increased supervision, and helping your child make more friends if he is isolated.

Ask your child what he has already tried to resolve the problem. Praise him for all the things he has tried. Give him permission to stop doing the things that haven't worked to stop the bullying. Encourage him to keep telling you and other adults. Help him to think about what has worked—or what *might* work. If your child is isolated, help him make connections through activities, hobbies, or clubs.

What if my child is in an abusive friendship with someone who hurts him or her? Both girls and boys sometimes get into friendships with someone who is a friend one day and mean the next, who talks behind their backs, and who makes them feel that this mean behavior is somehow their fault. The best way for young people to protect themselves from this hurt is to move on to other friendships, knowing that a real friend doesn't hurt you. Trudy Ludwig's wonderful book *My Secret Bully* (2003) is a great help in talking about this issue with young people.

How can I encourage my child to speak up about the bullying that he or she sees? Encourage your child to join with others in telling bullies to stop, telling adults when they see bullying, and reaching out in friendship to isolated youth. Praise your children when they do these things. Remind them that they have the power to help.

For more information: See the excellent pamphlet *Bullying Is Not a Fact of Life* on-line at http://www.mentalhealth.org/publications/allpubs/SVP-0052/.

APPENDIX C

GUIDING QUESTIONS FOR SUCCESSFUL RUBRIC DEVELOPMENT AND IMPLEMENTATION

—by Dee Lindenberger

1. Have all staff members helped define which types of peer-to-peer aggressive behaviors will be referred to the principal for action?

2. Have all staff members helped identify which types of peer-to-peer aggressive behaviors they will deal with themselves, unless those behaviors are frequent?

3. Is the rubric limited to and designed to address a broad range of peer-to-peer aggression (including the subcategory of bullying)? (Other forms of misbehavior, such as defiance to teachers or refusal to do schoolwork, should be handled separately.)

4. Does the rubric refer to specific, observable behaviors rather than the general terms *bullying* or *fighting?*

5. Are the behaviors described in the rubric clearly observable, rather than defined by intention or impact?

6. Are behaviors in the rubric divided into categories that escalate in severity (e.g., moderate– serious–severe or verbal–mild physical contact–severe physical contact)?

7. Does each category in the rubric include examples of behavior in addition to an open-ended statement that enables staff to address similar behaviors not specifically listed?

8. Are illegal behaviors, such as sexual or racial harassment, handled in accordance with law and district policy?

9. Are the consequences *fair*—beginning as small sanctions and escalating in accordance with the severity of the behavior?

10. Does the rubric use consequences that research has demonstrated to be effective (e.g., supervised inside recess, silent lunch, or in-school suspension)?

11. Do consequences avoid hidden rewards, such as attention from adults or avoidance of school time?

12. Is a guided reflection process included in the rubric as part of the consequence?

13. Does the rubric allow for development of an individualized plan for students who have special needs, are habitually aggressive, or do something that is beyond the scope of the rubric in severity or danger?

14. Is the discipline process implemented within a larger context of a positive feeling tone in the school?

15. Are adults positive role models who provide action-based praise for positive behavior and accomplishments, mentor high-risk students, and strive to create caring relationships with students?

16. Do all staff consistently report behaviors that are included in the rubric?

17. Are all students held equally accountable for their behavior, without consideration of special status or reputation (e.g., athletes, habitual offenders, "good" kids)?

18. Are there clear and posted standards of behavior for inside recess, suspension, and detention?

19. Are the investigation and reflection steps of the discipline process (including the application of consequences) conducted with a neutral feeling tone that conveys an undertone of caring and concern, as opposed to an emotional tone of hostility, frustration, intimidation, or punishment?

20. Do the individuals conducting the investigation and reflection steps ask open-ended questions to facilitate learning?

21. During the intervention process, do staff use language that encourages students to take full responsibility for their behaviors by describing the behaviors in simple, descriptive terms (e.g., "I heard that you hit him")?

22. Do staff avoid modifiers that relieve students of responsibility (e.g., "You seemed to have difficulty keeping your hands to yourself" or "I heard that you hit him because . . . .")?

23. Do staff acknowledge the student's positive intent and behavior during the investigation and reflection process (e.g., honesty, progress toward accepting responsibility, or sincere effort to reflect and learn)?

24. When the accused student denies responsibility and the event was not witnessed by an adult, are student witnesses interviewed one at a time?

25. Are there provisions to teach prosocial skills when it is obvious that the aggressive student needs additional help to learn alternative behaviors?

26. Are the three forms used for the discipline process (behavior report form, parent letter, reflection form) clear, easy to use, and designed to gather and impart all necessary information?

Annotated Bibliography and References

Aronson, E. (2000). *Nobody left to hate: Teaching compassion after Columbine.* New York: Owl Books.

Aronson describes useful strategies for developing an empathic, accepting school climate.

Baldwin, J. (1961). *Nobody knows my name.* New York: Random House.

Baumeister, R. F. (2001). Violent pride: Do people turn violent because of self-hate, or self-love? *Scientific American, 284*(4), 96–101.

Baumeister, R. F., Bushman, B. J., & Campbell, W. K. (2000). Self-esteem, narcissism, and aggression: Does violence result from low self-esteem or threatened egotism? *Current Directions in Psychological Science, 9,* 26–29.

Baumeister, R. F., Campbell, J. D., Krueger, J. I., & Vohs, K. D. (2003). Does high self-esteem cause better performance, interpersonal success, happiness, or healthier lifestyles? *Psychological Science in the Public Interest, 4,* 1–44. Retrieved August 1, 2006, from http://www.psy.fsu.edu/~baumeistertice/baumeisteretal2003.pdf

Baumeister, R. F., Twenge, J. M., & Nuss, C. (2002). Effects of social exclusion on cognitive processes: Anticipated aloneness reduces intelligent thought. *Journal of Personality and Social Psychology, 83,* 817–827.

Baumeister's work takes a clear, analytical look at the folklore our culture has developed about self-esteem.

Baumrind, D. (1966). Effects of authoritative parental control on child behavior. *Child Development, 37,* 887–907.

Baumrind, D. (1967). Child care practices anteceding three patterns of preschool behavior. *Genetic Psychology Monographs, 75,* 43–48.

Baumrind, D. (1996). The discipline controversy revisited. *Family Relations, 45,* 405–414.

Baumrind developed a way of understanding effective parenting that has influenced many people in this field.

Beane, A. (1999). *The bully-free classroom.* Minneapolis: Free Spirit.

Benard, B. (1995). *Fostering resilience in children* (ERIC Digest). Retrieved from http://www.ericfacility.net/databases/ERIC_Digests/ed386327.html

Clear statement of what works in fostering resiliency.

Block, P. (1999). *Flawless consulting: A guide to getting your expertise used.* San Francisco: Jossey-Bass/Pfeiffer.

A guide to having influence without having authority, for those of us in consulting or advising situations.

Bluestein, J. (2003). *What's wrong with I-messages?* Retrieved January 1, 2004, from http://www.janebluestein.com/Articles/Whatswrong.html

Highly recommended!

Bond L., Carlin, J. B., Thomas, L., Rubin, K., & Patton, G. (2001). Does bullying cause emotional problems? A prospective study of young teenagers. *British Medical Journal, 323,* 480–484.

Brendtro, L., Brokenleg, M., & Van Bockern, S. (1990). *Reclaiming youth at risk: Our hope for the future.* Bloomington, IN: National Educational Service.

This book's model of youth empowerment is based on contemporary developmental findings and Native American tradition.

Brown, L. M. (2003). *Girlfighting: Toward prevention.* Retrieved July 28, 2006, from http://www.hardygirlshealthywomen.org/docs/girlfighting_paper.doc

Brown, L. M. (2005). *Girlfighting: Betrayal and rejection among girls.* New York: University Press.

Brown's new curriculum, "From Adversaries to Allies: A Curriculum for Change," is now available from her organization, Hardy Girls, Healthy Women (http://www.hardygirlshealthywomen.org).

Brown, L. M. (2006). *Creating safe, responsive schools: Best-practices statement.* Retrieved August 8, 2006, from http://www.stopbullyingnow.com/Brown_safe_schools.pdf

Browne, A. (1989). *When battered women kill.* New York: Free Press.

Bunting, E. *A Day's Work, Fly Away Home, The Wednesday Surprise,* and other books. (several publishers)

Eve Bunting's children's books present altruism, empathy, and service to others in an engaging way.

Caplan, G. (1964). *Principles of preventive psychiatry.* New York: Basic Books.

Caplan's book presents a clear conceptualization of how to use knowledge about psychology to improve society.

Chasnoff, D. (2004). *Let's get real* [Video]. San Francisco: New Day Films.

Moving and articulate accounts about bullying from young people. Strongly recommended for staff training.

Cohn, A., & Canter, A. (2003). *Bullying: Facts for schools and parents.* Bethesda, MD: National Association of School Psychologists.

Useful general purpose pamphlet.

Connolly, J., Craig, W., Pepler, D., & Taradash, A. (2002). Dating experiences of bullies in early adolescence. *Child Maltreatment, 5,* 299–310.

Cotton, K. (1990). Schoolwide and classroom discipline. *School Improvement Research Series* (IClose-Up 9). Retrieved January 1, 2004, from http://www.nwrel.org/scpd/sirs/5/cu9.html

Craig, W., & Pepler, D. (2000a). *Making a difference in bullying* (LaMarsh Research Programme, Report 60). Retrieved January 18, 2004 from http://www.yorku.ca/lamarsh/ people/dpepler/ art_01.html

A detailed summary of research and interventions from the Canadian pioneers in bullying prevention.

Craig, W., & Pepler, D. (2000b). Observations of bullying in the playground and in the classroom. *School Psychology International, 21*(1), 22–37.

Crick, N. (2002). Bullies: Ignore them and they won't go away [Electronic version]. *The Link, 18*(2). Retrieved January 18, 2004, from http://education.umn.edu/alum/link/2002Winter/ bullies.html

Dake, J. A., Price, J. H., & Telljohann, S. (2003). The nature and extent of bullying at school. *Journal of School Health, 73*(5), 173–180.

Damon, W. (1995). *Greater expectations: Overcoming the culture of indulgence in America's homes and schools.* New York: Free Press.

Davis, N. (Ed.). (1999). *The U.S. Department of Health and Human Services' report on violence in schools.* Retrieved January 1, 2004, from http://www.mentalhealth.samhsa.gov/ schoolviolence/part1chp14.asp

Deci, E., & Flaste, R. (1996). *Why we do what we do: Understanding self-motivation.* New York: Penguin.

A clear view of human motivation and how to foster it.

DiCamillo, K. (2000). *Because of Winn-Dixie.* Cambridge, MA: Candlewick Press.

A good book to use for talking with students about how to make friends.

Dumas, J., & Nilsen, W. (2003). *Abnormal child and adolescent psychology.* Needham Heights, MA: Allyn and Bacon.

Thoughtful review of current research and interventions in child psychology.

Dweck, C. (2000). *Self-theories: Their role in motivation, personality, and development.* Philadelphia: Psychology Press.

Thirty years of research on young people's thought patterns that promote or discourage motivation. These are truly life-changing books.

Dweck, C. (2005) *Mindset: The new psychology of success.* New York: Random House.

Epstein, D. (1999). Effective intervention in domestic violence cases: Rethinking the roles of prosecutors, judges, and the court system. *Yale Journal of Law and Feminism, 11*(1), 3–50.

Eron, Huesmann, Dubo, Romanoff, & Yarnel (1987). Aggression and its correlates over 22 years. In D. H. Crowell & I. M. Evans (Eds.), *Childhood aggression and violence: Sources of influence, prevention, and control* (pp. 249–262). New York: Plenum.

Espelage, D. L. (2002). *Bullying in early adolescence: The role of the peer group* (ERIC Digest). Retrieved January 18, 2004, from http://ericcass.uncg.edu/virtuallib/bullying/1069.html

Estes, E. (1988). *The hundred dresses.* Orlando, FL: Voyager Books.

Well-written children's book, narrated from the point of view of a bystander. In my view, the best children's book about bullying.

Evanski, G. (2004). *Brain-compatible discipline with dignity.* Retrieved January 18, 2004, from http://www.disciplineassociates.com/printeditorial4.htm

Filcheck, H., McNeil, C., & Herschell, A. (2001). Types of verbal feedback that affect compliance and general behavior in disruptive and typical children. *Child Study Journal, 31*(4), 225–249.

Fisher, R., Patton, P., & Ury, W. (1983). *Getting to yes: Negotiating agreement without giving in.* New York: Penguin Books.

Revolutionary book about conflict resolution. This book is clear and to the point.

Friedman, S. (1996). *Peacemaking skills for little kids.* Miami: Peace Education Foundation, Inc. (Available from http://www.peaceeducation.com/curricula/)

Fun, effective curriculum for teaching nonviolence in kindergarten through second grade.

Garbarino, J. (1999). *Lost boys: Why our sons turn violent and how we can save them.* New York: Anchor Books.

Lessons from the author's work with teenage boys who have committed murder.

Garbarino, J. (2001). *Parents under siege: Why you are the solution, not the problem in your child's life.* New York: Free Press.

Authoritative and clear guide to raising children in a difficult time.

Garbarino, J., & DeLara, E. (2002). *And words can hurt forever.* New York: Free Press.

Highly recommended guide for parents of teens about stopping bullying.

Garfield, J. (1957). *Follow my leader.* New York: Vintage.

This novel talks about a young boy's experience with blindness and is useful in classrooms for talking about perseverance and disabilities.

Glasser, W. (1975). *Reality therapy: A new approach to psychiatry.* New York: HarperCollins.

Presents a revolutionary therapeutic approach focusing on taking responsibility for ourselves and understanding the effects our choices have on our lives.

Goleman, D. (1995). *Emotional intelligence.* New York: Bantam Books.

Groundbreaking work about understanding and building emotional competency.

Grandin, T. (1996). *Thinking in pictures—and other reports from my life with autism.* New York: Vintage.

Grandin's autobiography helps us see autism from the inside.

Gregoire, C. (2001). *Protecting our children: Attorney General's Task Force report on a legislative response to bullying.* Retrieved 1/18/04 from http://www.naag.org/features/bullying.php

Grossman, D. (2000, March 17). An interview with David Grossman: Giving children the skill and the will to kill. *The Executive Intelligence Review.* Retrieved July 26, 2006, from http://www.members.tripod.com/~american_almanac/grossint.htm

Haddon, M. (2004). *The curious incident of the dog in the night-time.* New York: Vintage.

This remarkable novel shows us the inner life of a young man with Asperger's syndrome.

Hartmann, T. (1997). *Attention deficit disorder: A different perception.* Nevada City, CA: Underwood Books.

A transforming book about ADD and the people who have it. This book asks, "What if we valued people who are always aware of everything in their environment and always able to shift their attention to the demands of the moment over people who plan ahead and work steadily toward tasks?"

Hazler, R. (1996). *Breaking the cycle of violence: Interventions for bullying and victimization.* Philadelphia: Taylor and Francis.

Practical strategies for helping youth who bully and targets of bullying.

Hoban, R., & Hoban, L. *Best Friends for Frances; A Bargain for Frances; Bread and Jam for Frances.* New York: HarperTrophy.

These endearing books present the normal dilemmas of childhood in a way that today's children can still connect with. The first two present friendship dilemmas that can lead to much productive discussion.

Horne, A. M., Bartolomucci, C. L., & Newman-Carlson, D. (2003). *Bully busters: A teacher's manual for helping bullies, victims, and bystanders (Grades 1-5).* Champaign, IL: Research Press.

Huesmann, L. R. (2002). *Study says TV violence influences children into adulthood.* Retrieved January 18, 2004, from www.kolr10.com/Global/story.asp?S=1173460&nav=0RXJEUqz

Huesmann, L. R., Moise-Titus, J., Podolski, C., & Eron, L. D. (2003). Longitudinal relations between children's exposure to TV violence and their aggressive and violent behavior in young adulthood: 1977–1992. *Developmental Psychology, 39*(2), 201–221.

Careful longitudinal research about the effects of television on young people.

Huntemann, H. (2000). *Game over: Gender, race, and violence in video games* [Video]. Northhampton, MA: Media Education Foundation. (Available from http://www.mediaed.org/videos/MediaGenderAndDiversity/GameOver)

Jewett Jarratt, C. (1994). *Helping children cope with separation and loss.* Cambridge, MA: Harvard Common Press.

Clear, concise, and built on a lifetime's work. Useful in dealing with all types of losses.

Jones, F. (2000). *Fred Jones tools for teaching.* Santa Cruz, CA: Fredric H. Jones and Associates.

The Fred Jones discipline and teaching materials are effective, research-based, and help teachers deal with the small and frequent disruptive behaviors that get in the way of instruction. See http://www.fredjones.com *for program details.*

The Josephson Institute of Ethics. (2000). *Report card on the ethics of American youth: Report 1. Violence, guns and alcohol.* Retrieved January 18, 2004, from http://www.charactercounts.org

Juvonen, J., Graham, S., & Schuster, M. (2003). Bullying among young adolescents: The strong, the weak, and the troubled. *Pediatrics, 112,* 1231–1237.

Kauffman, J. (1994). *Violence and aggression of children and youth: A call for action.* Retrieved January 18, 2004, from http://curry.edschool.virginia.edu/sped/projects/ose/papers/violence.html

Kay, M. (2004). *Disorders of written expression.* Retrieved August 1, 2006, from http://www.nldontheweb.org/Kay-1.htm

A summary of what is known about one of the "invisible" disabilities.

Kimmel, M. S., & Mahler, M. (2003). Adolescent masculinity, homophobia, and violence: Random school shootings, 1982–2001. *American Behavioral Scientist, 46*(10), 1439–1458.

Kimmel and Mahler write about bullying as a way young men enforce narrow gender role expectations and hurt male peers who do not fit those gender roles.

Knight, M. B. *Talking Walls; Africa Is Not a Country; Who Belongs Here: An American Story; Welcoming Babies; Talking Walls: The Stories Continue.* (several publishers).

Knight's warm, accessible books help young people think about their connections to each other.

Kohn, A. (1999). *Punished by rewards: The trouble with gold stars, incentive plans, A's, praise, and other bribes.* Boston: Houghton Mifflin.

Kohn presents the case for building intrinsic motivation.

Kohn, A. (2005). *Carrots or sticks? Alfie Kohn on rewards and punishment: An Education World wire-side chat.* Retrieved July 25, 2006, from http://www.educationworld.com/a_issues/chat/chat031.shtml (Originally published November 22, 2000; updated February 10, 2005)

Koppett, K. (2001). *Training to imagine.* Sterling, VA: Stylus Publishing.

Specific, useful ways to integrate theater techniques into effective teaching. Highly recommended!

Koss, A. G. (2002). *The girls.* New York: Puffin.

A story of girls' bullying, told from different points of view. Good for grades five to eight.

Lavoie, R. (n.d.) *The F.A.T. City Workshop Video.* Retrieved August 1, 2006, from http://www.ricklavoie.com/videos.html

Staff training tool to help educators understand the experience of having a learning disability.

Ludwig, T. (2003). *My secret bully.* Portland: Riverwood Press.

For upper elementary grades; an engaging, helpful children's book about relational aggression.

Mager, R., & Pipe, P. (1999). *Analyzing performance problems.* Atlanta: The Center for Effective Performance.

For supervisors who want to help staff change.

McCoy, E. (1997). *What to do . . . when kids are mean to your child.* Pleasantville, NY: Reader's Digest.

A clear and practical book for parents.

Miller, N. B., & Sammons, C. C. (1999). *Everybody's different: Understanding and changing our reactions to disabilities.* Baltimore: Brookes.

Full of practical advice for changing people's attitudes toward disabilities and the people who have them.

Moss, P. (2005). *Say something.* Gardiner, ME: Tilbury House.

This children's book is a useful resource for bystander training.

Mueller, C., & Dweck, C. (1998). Praise for intelligence can undermine children's motivation and performance. *Journal of Personality and Social Psychology, 75*(1), 33–52.

Mullin-Rindler, N. (1998). *Bully-proof: Quit it!* Wellesley, MA: Center for Research on Women.

Effective classroom curricula for empowering bystanders. These are the best I have seen in this field.

Mullin-Rindler, N. (2003). *Relational aggression and bullying: It's more than just a girl thing.* Wellesley, MA: Center for Research on Women.

Mynard, H., Joseph, S., & Alexander, J. (2000). Peer victimization and post-traumatic stress in adolescence. *Personality and Individual Differences, 29,* 815–821.

Nansel, T. R., Overpeck, M., Pilla, R. S., Ruan, W. J., Simons-Morton, B., & Scheidt, P. (2001). Bullying behaviors among U.S. youth: Prevalence and association with psychosocial adjustment. *The Journal of the American Medical Association, 285,* 2094–2100.

National Association of School Psychologists. (2002). *Bullying prevention: What schools and parents can do.* Bethesda, MD: National Association of School Psychologists. Retrieved January 18, 2004, from http://www.naspcenter.org/resourcekit/bullying_new_rk.html

National School Safety Center. (2001). *Review of school safety research.* Retrieved January 18, 2004, from http://www.nssc1.org/studies/statistic%20resourcespdf.pdf

Nelesen, A. (2003, April 8). 3 Green Bay teens get jail time for beating classmate. *Green Bay Press Gazette.* Retrieved May 30, 2005, from http://www.greenbaypressgazette.com/news/archive/local_9666907.shtml

Newman, K. (2004). *RAMPAGE: The social roots of school shootings.* New York: Basic Books.

Indispensable resource to help us prevent future school shootings.

Newman-Carlson, D. A., Horne, A. M., & Bartolomucci, C. L. (2000). *Bully busters: A teacher's manual for helping bullies, victims, and bystanders (Grades 6–8)*. Champaign, IL: Research Press.

New South Wales Health Department. (2001). *What parents should know about bullying*. Retrieved January 18, 2004, from http://www.mhcs.health.nsw.gov.au/ health-public-affairs/mhcs/publications/5705.html

Northwest Regional Educational Laboratory. (2001). *Schoolwide prevention of bullying*. Retrieved January 18, 2004, from http://www. nwrel.org/request/dec01/bullying.pdf

A clear description of what works and what doesn't.

Ohio Legal Rights Service. (n.d.). *What can I do if my child with a disability is being harassed in school?* Retrieved May 30, 2005, from http://olrs.ohio.gov/ASP/olrs/SpecEd2.asp

Olweus, D. (1993). *Bullying at school: What we know and what we can do*. Malden, MA: Blackwell Publishers.

Olweus, D. (2000). *Teacher handbook: Olweus's core program against bullying and antisocial behavior.* (Available from http://www.clemson.edu/olweus/)

Olweus, D. (2003a). *Bullying is not a fact of life*. Retrieved July 27, 2006, from http://www.mentalhealth.samhsa.gov/media/ ken/pdf/SVP-0052/SVP-0052.pdf 2003

Olweus, D. (2003b). A profile of bullying at school. *Educational Leadership, 60*(6), 12–17.

Olweus's work is the foundation of modern bullying prevention.

Olweus, D., Limber, S., & Mihalic, S. (1997). *Blueprints for violence prevention: Bullying prevention program*. Denver: C & M Press.

O'Neill, D. L., & Glass, B. A. (2000). *Kelso's choice: Conflict management skills*. Elgin, IL: Sunburst.

A practical conflict management curriculum for K–5.

Parsons, L. (2005). *Bullied teacher: Bullied student—How to recognize the bullying culture in your school and what to do about it.* Portland, ME: Stenhouse Publishers.

Paterson, K. (1987). *The Great Gilly Hopkins; Bridge to Terabithia.* New York: HarperTrophy.

Paterson writes with a deep honesty about children's emotions, reminding us that young people face dilemmas that are as serious as adults'.

Payne, R. (2001). *A framework for understanding poverty.* Highlands, TX: Aha! Press.

Pennebaker, J. (1997). *Opening up: The healing power of expressing emotions.* New York: Guilford.

Research about the positive effects of journaling.

Perlstein, L. (2003). *Not Much Just Chillin': The Hidden Lives of Middle Schoolers.* New York: Farrar, Straus & Giroux.

This breathtaking book takes us inside middle schoolers' lives and shows us what adults can—and shouldn't—do.

Peterson, K. (1998). *Establishing effective schoolwide behavior management and discipline systems* (Reform Talk, 10). Wisconsin Center for Education Research (WCER), School of Education, University of Wisconsin–Madison. Retrieved January 18, 2004, from http://www.wcer.wisc.edu/ccvi/pub/ReformTalk/Year_1998/Oct_98_Reform_Talk_10.html

Piazza, N. *The rules of counseling.* Retrieved January 18, 2004, from http://cmhs.utoledo.edu/npiazza/Humor/Rules.htm

This set of maxims for counselors contains much wisdom learned from professional experience.

Plohetski, T. (2003, January 16). 5 teens charged in taped assault group beat special education student at bus stop, police say. *American-Statesman.* Retrieved May 30, 2005, from http://www.bridges4kids.org/articles/1-03/AS1-16-03.html

Rigby, K. (2000). Effects of peer victimisation in schools and perceived social support on adolescent well-being. *Journal of Adolescence, 23*(1), 57–68.

Rock, E., Hammond, M., & Rasmussen, S. (2002). *School program to teach empathy and bully prevention.* Retrieved January 18, 2004, from http://ericcass.uncg.edu/virtuallib/bullying/1071.html

Rohd, M. (1998). *Hope is vital: Theater for community, conflict, and dialogue.* Portsmouth, NH: Heinemann.

A specific and helpful book about using theater in education and social change.

Roland, E., & Galloway, D. (2002). Classroom influences on bullying. *Educational Research, 44*(3), 299–312.

Roosevelt, E. (1958, March 27). Remarks at presentation of booklet on human rights, *In your hands,* to the United Nations Commission on Human Rights, New York.

Ross, D. (1996). *Childhood bullying and teasing.* Alexandria, VA: American Counseling Association Press.

The first research-based American book about bullying. Clear work by a pioneer of American psychology.

Rutter, M., Giller, H., & Hagell, A. (1998). *Antisocial behavior by young people.* Cambridge, UK: Cambridge University Press.

A wide range of research, all critically evaluated. A vital resource!

Sacks, O. (1996). *An anthropologist on Mars: Seven paradoxical tales.* New York: Vintage Books.

Sacks, O. (1998). *The man who mistook his wife for a hat: And other clinical tales.* New York: Touchstone.

Sacks's sensitive casebooks help us see the inner world of people whose perceptions and lives are different from ours.

Safe Schools Fact Sheets: Bullying—an overview of bullying. Retrieved January 18, 2004, from http://www.colorado.edu/ cspv/publications/factsheets/

Salmivalli, C., Lagerspetz, K., Bjorkvist, K., Osterman, K., & Kaukiainen, A. (1996). Bullying as a group process: Participant roles in their relations to social satus within the group. *Aggressive Behavior, 22*(1), 1–15.

Sanford, L. (1992). *Strong at the broken places.* New York: Avon.

An inspiring analysis of how people recover from trauma.

Second Step: A violence prevention curriculum. Available from Committee for Children, 568 First Avenue South, Suite 600, Seattle, WA 98104–2804. (Ordering details at http://www.cfchildren.org/)

Seuss, Dr. (1940). *Horton hatches the egg.* New York: Random House Books for Young Readers.

Good book to use to help young children discuss responsibility.

Sharp, S., & Smith, P. (Eds.). (1994). *Tackling bullying in your schools.* New York: Routledge.

Full of detailed, practical techniques and interventions.

Shepard, J. (2004). *Project X.* New York: Knopf.

This frightening novel takes us inside the mind of a boy who has been humiliated by peers and who chooses to respond violently.

Sherman, L. W., Denise, G., MacKenzie, D., Eck, J., Reuter, P., & Bushway, S. (1997). *Preventing crime: What works, what doesn't, what's promising: A report to the United States Congress.* Prepared for the National Institute of Justice, University of Maryland, Office of Justice Programs. Retrieved January 18, 2004, from http://www.preventingcrime.org/report/index.htm

Shreve, S. R. (1993). *Joshua T. Bates takes charge.* New York: Knopf.

While this book's plot may be a bit contrived, it opens up discussion of boy-to-boy teasing based on the beginnings of homophobia.

Shure, M. B. (2000a). Bullies and their victims: A problem-solving approach to prevention. *Brown University Child and Adolescent Behavior Letter, 16,* 1, 6.

Shure, M. B. (2000b). *Raising a thinking child workbook: Teaching young children how to resolve everyday conflicts and get along with others.* Champaign, IL: Research Press.

Shure, M. B. (2001a). *I Can Problem Solve (ICPS): An interpersonal cognitive problem-solving program* (Preschool). Champaign, IL: Research Press.

Shure, M. B. (2001b). *I Can Problem Solve (ICPS): An interpersonal cognitive problem-solving program* (Kindergarten and Primary Grades). Champaign, IL: Research Press.

Shure, M. B. (2001c). *I Can Problem Solve (ICPS): An interpersonal cognitive problem-solving program* (Intermediate Elementary Grades). Champaign, IL: Research Press.

Shure, M. B. (2001d). What's right with prevention? Commentary on "prevention of mental disorders in school-aged children: current state of the field" (Article 7). *Prevention and Treatment, 4.* (Online at http://www.journals.apa.org/prevention/volume4/pre0040007c.html)

Shure, M. B., & Spivack, G. (1982). Interpersonal problem-solving in young children: A cognitive approach to prevention. *American Journal of Community Psychology, 10,* 341–356.

Shure's work is an indispensable resource for teaching children to solve problems and think about life.

Simmons, A. (2002). *Odd girl out: The hidden culture of aggression in girls.* Orlando, FL: Harcourt.

A description of relational aggression.

Smith, B., Steinem, G., & Mink, G. (Eds.). (1998). *The reader's companion to U.S. women's history.* Boston: Houghton Mifflin. Retrieved January 18, 2004, from http://college.hmco.com/history/readerscomp/women/html/w m_033700_sexualharass.htm

Starr, L. (2000). Bullying intervention strategies that work. *Education World.* Retrieved January 18, 2004, from http://www.educationworld.com/a_issues/issues103.shtml

Steig, W. (1988). *Brave Irene.* New York: Farrar, Strauss and Giroux.

An opportunity to discuss courage and disappointment with young people.

Sutherland, K., Wehby, J., & Copeland, S. (2000). Effect of varying rates of behavior-specific praise on the on-task behavior of students with EBD. *Journal of Emotional and Behavioral Disorders, 8*(1), 2–9.

Sweeting, H., & West, P. (2001) Being different: Correlates of the experience of teasing and bullying at age 11. *Research Papers in Education, 16*(3), 225–246.

Taffel, R. (1999). *Nurturing good children now.* New York: Golden Books.

Taffel, R. (2001a). *Getting through to difficult kids and parents: Uncommon sense for child professionals.* New York: Guilford.

Taffel, R. (2001b). *The second family: How adolescent power is challenging the American family.* New York: St. Martin's Press.

These books present creative and effective strategies for parenting and for working with families.

Thorne, B. (1993) *Gender play: Girls and boys in school.* New Brunswick, NJ: Rutgers University Press.

U.S. Department of Education. (2000). *Letter to schools about disability harassment.* Retrieved March 15, 2005, from

http://www.ed.gov/PressReleases/072000/
PolicyDisabilityharassment.doc

A clear statement of the importance of stopping disability harassment.

U.S. Department of Health and Human Services. (2003). *Bullying is not a fact of life.* Retrieved February 22, 2004, from http://www.mentalhealth.org/publications/allpubs/ SVP-0052/

U.S. Department of Justice, Office on Violence against Women. (n.d.) *Civil rights for women.* Retrieved January 18, 2004, from http://www.ojp.usdoj.gov/vawo/laws/vawa/stitle_c.htm

Vaillancourt, T., Hymel, S., & McDougall, P. (2003). Bullying is power: Implications for school-based intervention strategies. *Journal of Applied School Psychology, 19*(2), 157–176.

Voors, W. (2003). Bullying—both sides of the fence. *Paradigm, 8*(1) & *6*(4), 16.

Weber, M. C. (2002). Disability harassment in the public schools. *William and Mary Law Review, 43*(3), 1085–1157.

A detailed review of the legal issues in disability harassment.

Wessler, S. L. (2003). *The respectful school: How educators and students can conquer hate and harassment.* Alexandria, VA: Association for Supervision and Curriculum Development.

Outstanding book by the originator of Maine's student civil rights teams and director of the University of Maine's Center for the Prevention of Hate Violence.

Wylie, M. S. (2000). Teaching kids to care. *Family Therapy Networker, 24*(5), 26–35.

Yoon, J., & Kerber, K. (2003). Bullying: Elementary teachers' attitudes and intervention strategies. *Research in Education, 69,* 27–35.

ABOUT THE AUTHOR

Stan Davis has worked for human rights in many different ways. In the 1960s he marched with Dr. King in the South and worked for civil rights in the North. Since 1969, he has worked as a family and child therapist with abused and grieving children and trained child protective workers and other helping professionals. He designed and implemented training for a network of rape crisis centers and helped police develop effective interventions for domestic abuse. He has been active in community conflict resolution and crisis intervention.

In the 1980s he became a school counselor. Since the mid-1990s, he has focused his energies on helping schools prevent bullying. He works part-time in an elementary school in Maine and trains and consults with educators nationwide as well. Stan has trained school staff all over the United States. His strategies are part of statewide initiatives in Michigan, New Jersey, and West Virginia. Stan's work has been featured in national newspaper and radio articles and on a special *20/20* report on bullying with ABC news reporter John Stossel. Stan has a B.A. in psychology from Brown University and is certified as a social worker and a school counselor. He is a certified Olweus Bullying Prevention Program consultant and a founding member of the International Bullying Prevention Association.